BEING THE APPROVED, VERIFIED, SYMPAT

EGYPTIAN SECRETS

OR

WHITE AND BLACK ART FOR MAN AND BEAST

> "The Book of Nature and the Hidden Secrets and Mysteries of Life Unveiled; Being the Forbidden Knowledge of Ancient Philosophers by that celebrated Student, Philosopher, Chemist, Naturalist, Psychomist, Astrologer, Alchemist, Metallurgist, Sorcerer, Explanator of the Mysteries of Wizards and Witchcraft; together with recondite Views of numerous Arts and Science—Obscure, Plain, Practical, etc."

This book reveals Magical Formulas for Health, Protection, Power, Victory, Medicines, etc.

Albertus Magnus

ISBN 1-56459-356-8

> Request our FREE CATALOG of over 1,000
> # Rare Esoteric Books
> ## Unavailable Elsewhere
>
> Alchemy, Ancient Wisdom, Astronomy, Baconian, Eastern-Thought, Egyptology, Esoteric, Freemasonry, Gnosticism, Hermetic, Magic, Metaphysics, Mysticism, Mystery Schools, Mythology, Occult, Philosophy, Psychology, Pyramids, Qabalah, Religions, Rosicrucian, Science, Spiritual, Symbolism, Tarot, Theosophy, *and many more!*

Kessinger Publishing Company
Montana, U.S.A.

ALBERTUS MAGNUS

BEING THE APPROVED, VERIFIED, SYMPATHETIC AND NATURAL

EGYPTIAN SECRETS

OR,

WHITE AND BLACK ART FOR MAN AND BEAST

THE BOOK OF NATURE AND THE HIDDEN SECRETS AND MYSTERIES OF LIFE UNVEILED; BEING THE

Forbidden Knowledge of Ancient Philosophers

By that celebrated Student, Philosopher, Chemist, Naturalist, Psychomist, Astrologer, Alchemist, Metallurgist, Sorcerer, Explanator of the Mysteries of Wizards and Witchcraft; together with recondite Views of numerous Arts and Sciences—Obscure, Plain, Practical, Etc., Etc.

TRANSLATED FROM THE GERMAN

CONTENTS OF VOL. I.

To secure Men and Beasts against Evil Spirits—To become Strong—To Stop the Blood—When Suffering from Burns—For the Wild Fire—For the Sweeny Disease—For Cramps—For Worms—For all kinds of Fevers—For Colic—to Heal Ruptures of Young and Aged People—For Epilepsy—For Scabs—For Putrid Mouths—For Sore Eyes—For Erysipelas—For Pestilence—When a Child is Liver Grown—For Consumptive Lungs—For Gravel—For Dysentery—For Cancer—How to detect a Thief—For the Gout—For Arthritis—For Sore Breasts—How to Recover Stolen Property—To make a Thief own up—For Hysterics—To Prevent Danger of Fire from your House—To Secure a House so that no Fire will ever go eat therein—How to Quench Fire—For Toothache—For the Itch—For Bad Hearing—To Destroy Bed Bugs—To make an Incombustible Oil—To drive away Spiders and House Flies—To Destroy Rats and Mice—A Curious Performance to Improve Common Wine, and make the same Good in a quick way—How to make Wine Good and Wholesome—To make Wine Clear in a quick manner—To Discern all Diseases by examining the Water—For Hydrophobia, and many other Approved Wonderful Performances, hitherto unknown, and now printed for the Benefit of Mankind, for the first time.

EGYPTIAN PUBLISHING CO.

CHICAGO.

TO THE KIND READER.

I HEREWITH commit to the perusal of the reader a collection of approved remedies—sympathetic as well as natural—remedies, sufficient in number as may be deemed needful for household purposes. Knowing, from experience, how many an honest citizen hath been robbed of his entire estate through the machination of bad and malicious people, having his live stock destroyed and the usefulness of his cows tampered with; and still further, how many a man hath been tortured and tantalized at night, from early childhood, by wicked people of that ilk; so much so that they could hardly bear it any longer, had it not been for the timely aid rendered them by exorcising these rabbles, if this be even done by calling upon the Bedgoblin or "Puck." Moveover, many such troubled people were made unhappy in their wedlock, and robbed of all their children. Besides all this I know of a place, of which the minister of the Gospel who officiates there assures me, that the influence of but one wicked female residing there has caused the ruin of the entire village, since there is hardly man or beast existing in the place which had not been tampered with and attacked by that wicked person. But, through the grace of God, every one of these people have been rescued by the means of the Bedgoblin, as set forth in the second article of this little book.

Whenever said remedy is to be applied, in case the house of him whom it is intended to assist is called aloud three times with devotion, and by adding both his christian and all his other names, the usefulness thereof will be readily enough perceived, the matrimonial peace will be re-established, the children will recover, the cows will again become useful, no matter how much reduced in body they have been; but a few weeks will elapse, and the cows will show as much sound flesh as they ever possessed heretofore. Thus it happens that this collection contains a number of curious performances of magic, every one of which is worth far more than the reader pays for this entire book.

For the purpose of rendering a great service to mankind, this book was issued, in order to bridle and check the doings of the Devil.

Whatever objections may be raised against this book by disbelief and jealousy, these pages will, despite all such objections, contain naught else but truth divine, since Christ himself hath commanded that all ye may perform, ye shall do in the name of God, the Son and the Holy Spirit, so that the Devil may not possess any power over anything whatsoever to do his will; and it will thus happen unto many persons, as was experienced by Job, who, having lost his fortune and his children, by his endurance and perseverance in the belief of God, and the blessings of the good deeds which were performed by him every day, Job wrested the power from the Devil, and he afterward became wealthier than he ever was before. Thus we also must act, that is, bless our possessions, our homes, and entrust them to the care of the Lord, and doubtless the Devil will have to retire and succumb.

I, therefore, beseech every one, into whose hands this book may come, not to treat the same lightly or to destroy the same, because, by such action, he will defy the will of God, and God will, in return therefore destroy him, and cause him to suffer eternal punishment and grim damnation. But to him who properly esteems and values this book, and never abuses its teachings, will not only be granted the usefulness of its contents, but he will also attain everlasting joy and blessing.

Now remains merely to add a note: Wherever the "2 N. N." occurs, both the baptismal name and all other names of him whom you intend to help, aid or assist, will have to be added, while the † † † signify the highest name of God, which should always be added in conclusion. Every sympathetic formula should be repeated three times.

And now, I submit this book to you, dear reader, for your best use and profit, in the name of God the Father, the Son, and the Holy Spirit. Amen! Yea, even so be it.

ALBERTUS MAGNUS

OR

EGYPTIAN SECRETS

If a Human Being or Beast is attacked by Evil Spirits. how to restore him and make him well again.

Thou arch-sorcerer, thou has attacked N. N.; let that witchcraft recede from him into thy marrow and into thy bone, let it be returned unto thee. I exorcise thee for the sake of the five wounds of Jesus, thou evil spirit, and conjure thee for the five wounds of Jesus of this flesh, marrow and bone; I exorcise thee for the sake of the five wounds of Jesus, at this very hour restore to health again N. N., in the name of God the Father, God the Son, and of God the Holy Spirit. Three times.

If a Man or Beast is attacked by Wicked People, and how to banish them forever from the House so that they may never be able to do any Harm.

Bedgoblin and all ye evil spirits, I forbid you my bedstead, my couch; I forbid you, in the name of God, my house and home; I forbid you, in the name of the Holy Trinity, my blood and flesh, my body and soul; I forbid you all the nail holes in my house and home, till you have traveled over every hillock, waded through every water, have counted all the leaflets of the trees, and counted all the starlets in the sky, until that beloved day arrives when the mother of God will bring forth her second Son. † † †

This formula, three times spoken in the house of the person whom we seek to aid, always adding, in the right place, both his baptismal and other names, has been found excellent in many hundred cases.

For Gangrene or Mortification.

Christ the Lord went through the field, and met a person who was sick of palsy. Christ the Lord spake: Whither art thou going, thou cold face? The face thus addressed replied: I will enter into that man. Christ the Lord said: What wilt thou do in the body of that man? I will shatter his bones to death, eat his flesh, and drink his blood. Christ the Lord sayeth: Thou palsied face, thou shalt not do so; pebble stones thou must devour, bitter herbs thou shalt pluck; from a well thou must drink, and therein shalt thou sink. † † †

On a Friday it was, when our Lord was tortured. As this is the case, so may Christ deliver me from Cramp, from palsy, and apparition. In the second place, thou shalt stand quietly, half of the back, shank or leg, or any other limb or member, I may possess on my body, be the same dull, blind, pliable or pliant; therefore, cramp, palsy or apparition, thou canst go no further, such commandeth unto thee the man who suffered death upon the cross as Jesus Christ; He who by His bitter tortures and by His death hath been sacrificed. All may move—foliage and grasses, all things which upon earth do grow, as also our dear Master Jesus Christ's water and blood; that he may do unto all believing Christian people, who bent themselves on account of His great nature, while the holy body hung on His Cross. Therefore, the Jews spake: Master, thou didst first comfort the cramp, the palsy and the apparition; but Jesus replied: Cramp, palsy and apparitions I do not have. Be it woman or man; so help me Christ, the joy and comfort of the sacred cross of Him who is arisen out of corruption's womb; burst ye the spell, break from your gloom! By the joy He caused unto His mother, Jesus of Nazareth, God be merciful to me, a poor sinner. † † †

Whoever carries this letter with him on his person, so as to be enabled to recite the same at will, will never more of cramp, palsy or apparition become ill.

For Gangrene of Man or Beast.

Three lords are riding between two ladies. The first is called St. Luke, the other St. Mark, the third St. John. They hold forth their arm, bless that face so warm; extend their hands, bless the face so charmingly; they stretch out their thumbs, they bless Sodoma. † † † Three times, and the Lord's Prayer.

For the Worm on any part of the Limb, wherever it may be.

Worm, I conjure thee, by the beams of sacred daylight; worm, I conjure thee, by the mystic shades of night; worm, I conjure thee by those five wounds; worm, I conjure thee by those holy three nails of Christ; worm, I conjure thee, by the power of God Almighty, if thou be green, blue, white, black or red, that thou shalt now be lying in the finger stark and dead, and may this be counted as penance for thee. † † † Three times to be recited, and every time the holiest name of the Lord is repeated, blow over the diseased limb.

For the Worms in the Body.

God went upon an acre field, upon red acre land. He made three furrows, and found three worms. The first was black, the other was white, the third was red; forthwith N. N. all thy worms are dead. † † † Move three times with the finger around the navel, while pronouncing the three holiest names.

For the Worm on Limb or Member.

Take fresh ox gall, heat it, and dip the limb or member thus affected therein. Use the mixture as hot as you are able to bear it. The worm will die.

For Griping Pain or Colic.

An old tuft head, an old body coat, a glass of rue wine; bowels, cease thy griping pain. Three times. Excellent!

For Fever.

Nut tree, I come unto thee; take the seventy-seven fevers from me. I will persist therein. † † †

This must be written upon a scrap of paper, and, with the same, hie to a nut tree ere the sun rises. Cut a piece of the bark, insert the paper under it, recite the above sentence three times, and put the bark in its place again, so that it may grow together.

To transplant the Rupture of a Young Man.

Cut three tufts of hair from the centre of his head; tie the same in a clean cloth, carry it into another district, (county), and bury it under a young willow tree, so that it may grow together. † † † Proved.

For the Sweeny in all Limbs and Members of Man or Beast.

N. N., (these N.'s signify the names of him whom we intend to help, and these will have to be called, then speak:) thou swinest in thy flesh; thou swinest in thy blood. N. N., (here again, both baptismal and family names are pronounced,) sloth leave thy marrow; sloth leave thy bone; sloth leave thy nerve; sloth leave thy blood; sloth be removed from thy skin. N. N. sloth, go into the wild sea, where neither man nor beast may be, and be not able to multiply. † † †

Another Remedy for the Sweeny.

Shank leg swine, as God the Father; shank leg swine, as God the son; shank leg swine, as God the Holy Spirit! Shank leg (or arm) swine, be prone, like stone. † † † Three times.

For Erysipelas or St. Anthony's Fire.

I strolled through a red forest, and in the red forest there was a red church, and in the red church stood a red Altar, and upon the red altar there lay a red knife; take the red knife and cut red bread. † † †

For Epilepsy or Fits.

Take some part of the hind leg of a calf, also part of a bone of a human body, from a graveyard; pulverize both, mix the mass well, and give the patient three points of a knife full. If a person is attacked by this disease, and falls upon the ground, you must let him lie and not touch him. † † †

For Scabs.

At the burial of any person, proceed to a running stream, and draw water from it with your hands, and pour it over the head. While the water runs downward, draw the water also downward; and whenever the water is poured upon the head, do not cease to utter: Call, recede and leave, like the dead in the grave.

This ought to be done during the chiming or tolling of the funeral bells, without much noise. Water must be continualy drawn during the tolling of the bells.

For the Haish.

Three maidens went helter-skelter, hurry, click, over mountains and hillocks, mighty quick. The first spake: The filly has the haish. The other said: It has it not. The third ejaculated: It has it. † † †

To prevent Scars or Pock Marks to remain when a Person has received Burns on any Limb or Member of the Body.

St. Lawrence sat upon his steed. God, the Lord, bless his burns, that they may not grow deep into the flesh, and eat into his body fresh. In the name of God the Father, God the Son, and God the Holy Ghost. Amen.

Three times spoken, and each time, while repeating the three holy names, must be blown over the burns, from the body outwards.

For the Wild Fire of Man and Beast.

Wild fire, wild burning, aching and pain, curdled blood and gangrene, God embrace thee. The Lord save thee. God is the most Supreme Being. He is alone able to dispel and drive away wild fire, gangrene, erysipelas and curdled blood; also, do away with all your sores, with all that pains you. Three times to be spoken, and each time blowing the three highest attributes of divinity over the wounds.

For Burns.

Away burns, undo the band; if cold or warm, cease the hand. God save thee, N. N.; thy flesh, thy blood, thy marrow, thy bone, and all thy veins. They all shall be saved, for warm and cold brands reign. † ☦ † Three times spoken.

Another Remedy for the Same Ailment.

Our Lord Jesus Christ and St. Peter walked over the field. They saw and smelt a wild, hot fiery brand. Christ, with his powerful hand quenched N. N. his wild, hot, fiery brand, so that no longer fire is sent, and friendly becomes that element, just like our dear matron's child again became well. † † † Three times.

An Ointment for Burns.

Take lime; slake it off with water drawn from a brook whilst running downward. One-half water and the other half linseed oil. After this, add a small piece of white lead, ground fine. Render it to the subsistence of a salve.

To Still the Blood.

Three blissful hours are to this world bestowed. In the first of these hours God was born, in the other hour God died, in the other hour, however, God was resurrected. Now, I call the three blissful hours, and quiet thee, N. N., so that thy water and thy blood may be healed from all ailment and wounds, and henceforth may thou in health abound. † † † Three times.

For Swellings.

Swelling, swelling, swelling, in the name of Jesus, I command thee, that thou shalt cause N. N., as little pain as the three nails caused our Saviour Jesus Christ. Those nails were driven through his hands and feet by the wicked Jews. † † † Three times.

The salves for burns and sores are likewise applied for worms and swelling.

Still Another Remedy for Swellings.

Blissful be the day, blissful be that hour, when thou wilt neither be smitten with swellings or boils, till the Virgin Mary with another son will toil. † † †

For a Putrid Mouth.

Job, Job, traveled through the land; he carried a rod in his smitten hand; then God, the Lord, in a vision did appear, and spake: Job, Job, why mournest thou, my dear? Lord, why should I not feel very sad, since wild and putrid is the tongue and the mouth of my child. † † † Three times.

Wash for a Putrid Mouth.

Take of refined white vitriol, five cents worth. Dissolve in a quart of water, and dip a clean rag therein, wherewith to wash the mouth.

When a Bone is Wrenched, Dislocated or Sprained. (For Man and Beast.)

A deer ran over a meadow to graze. He went to his green, grazing place, when, lo! he sprained his leg upon a stone. But Jesus, the Lord, beheld the scene, and healed, with ointment of lard and fat, his sore, and swiftly the deer ran, as fast as before.

Another Remedy for the same Trouble.

I or you have sprained the leg. They have crucified Jesus upon the cross. If to Him crucifixion caused no pain, thy leg will not be hurt from this sprain. † † † Three times.

For Sore Eyes.

Blissful and holy is the day on which Christ, the Lord, was born, fly away my blindness. Logoo-maloo, the wicked blind Jew, who pierced the Saviour's side through and through; from this stab issued water and blood, which for N. N.'s eyes will be very wholesome and good. † † †

When an Animal treads on a Nail, speak thus:

This is the nail which was used to nail Christ, the Lord; that it may not swell or fester, and no other injury may cause. † † †

For Wounds and Stopping of Blood.

Blessed is the day on which Jesus Christ was born; blessed is the day on which Jesus Christ died; blessed is the day on which Jesus Christ arose from the dead. These are holy three hours; by these, N. N., I stop thy blood. Thy sores shall neither swell nor fester; no more shall that happen, than that the Virgin Mary will bear another son. † † †

To Stop the Blood.

Upon Christ's grave three lilies grow. The first is named **Youth**; the other, **Virtue's Truth**; the third, **SUBUL. Blood stop.** † † †

When an Animal has Gangrene.

Mix a shot of gun-powder with the water, and let the animal take it. It will certainly derive benefit therefrom.

When the Milk leaves a Cow.

Take a new earthen vessel, for which you must pay without bartering. In this dish place the water of such an afflicted cow, whilst calling the three highest names; also put a knife, with three cents, in the dish. Thereupon put the dish in a locked chest, and this chest again in another larger chest, and the latter in a trough, so that the earthen vessel is closed up by three locks. If, after this, somebody calls to obtain something from you, do not give it to him.

For the Erysipelas of Animals.

Write upon a paper as follows, and give it with the food to the cattle: Three virgin maidens went over the land. One carries a piece of bread in the hand. The one said: we will divide it and cut it; the other spake: we will heal the erysipelas of N. N.'s cow. † † †

Three times spoken, written upon a piece of paper, and, in a bit of bread, given to the cow.

When a Person, Adult or Child is Swelled.

Take a handful of crowfoot, daisies with or without the roots, one white onion, with the skin, a handful of cimprefoil, cut all these fine and mix together, then take four ounces of butter, made of goat milk, which must be melted in these articles, and boil the herbs. Believe it long. Press this through a cloth, stir it like lard, let it stand awhile. Apply it to the person that has the swelling, by greasing the same from the pit of the stomach, around the ribs, several times.

For Impure Air.

Take three shrubs of rue, three of hazlenut, and three of junipers. Fumigate with these.

To know when Cattle are Plagued by Witches.

The hair stand on end, or bristles on the head, and they generally sweat by night or near dawn of day.

EGYPTIAN SECRETS.

How to cause that a Cow will not bear a Steer, but a Cow Calf.

Take the purification of the cow, when it calves, and bury it under an apple tree, then she will bear a cow-calf the next time.

When Pestilence rages among the Cattle.

Take juniper vinegar, teriac and powder of rosemary roots, a grip full thereof mixed with the teriac and vinegar, and pour out as a drink to the cattle, and then let them fast for three hours.

That no Ill may befall the Cattle.

Whenever you bake, you should give them the slake water to drink, and naught will happen to them.

How to Wean Calves.

On the third day before full moon, this should be done, and splendid large cattle will be the result.

When the Udder and the Stroke of a Cow are Sore.

Take radish leaves, pound them in a mortar, press them out, and apply this to the udder and stroke with a feather.

When Cattle Swell Up.

Scrape from your finger nails as much as possible with a knife, and give it to your cattle, with bread. Very sure.

When Cattle or Horses' Jawbone is Set.

Take the three fingers used in swearing an oath, put them into the mouth of the animal and speak: Hep hada, Hep hada, Hep hada, open thyself. † † † Three times.

When Cattle is Bewitched.

Take witchcraft balsam, glow worm oil, black juniper berry, oil of rue, oil of turpentine, two cents worth of each. Give this mixture to the cattle; also, some balsam of sulphur.

When a person is troubled with a tumor or desires to remove Corns.

When they bury an old man, and the funeral bells are ringing, the following should be spoken: they are sounding the funeral bell and what I now grasp may soon be well and what ill I grasp do take away, like the dead one in the grave does lay. † † † Whilst reciting the sentence, always hold the troubled part in the hand, and regarding the corns, move over them with your fingers after cutting out the corns, and as long as they are tolling the bells repeat the above. As soon as the dead body begins to bleach the tumor or the corns will disappear. Probate in the case of a male, wait for the funeral of one of that sex; in the case of a female wait until a female is to be buried.

When a Sore fails to Break open.

Take virgin-parchments as large as the sore, put it first in water and then on the sore spot. Propatum!

For Swelling of the Body.

Take wheat flour, eggs, saffron, vinegar, and mix it into a salve. Apply the same as a poultice. Excellent.

An Ointment for Consumptive Limbs.

Take lard of bear, fox and badger, tallow of a deer, juniper berry, oleum philosophorum and some soap, of each two ounces, and mix a handful of corimon nettle chopped very fine, boil in wine to the thickness of a salve or ointment. Apply to the afflicted member often mornings and evenings. Approved.

For the Engerling in Sheep.

Mix speedwell among the salt when feeding, and the sheep will neither rot nor die. Approved.

For One who cannot hold his Water.

Take talons of a buck, burn them to powder and give it in a beverage to the afflicted.

When a Cow has lost her Milk.

Milk the cow upon the bottom of the tub, put the tub in a safe place, so that nothing can be added to its contents, take a knife wherewith to draw a cross through the milk, and dip it three times into the milk. Keep the tub with the milk in safety. Continue this for several days in succession.

When a Cow, after having Calved, will not cleanse herself.

Take hazlewort with the herb, cut it fine, and give it to the cow in water or wine; or you may give the cow a handful of wintergreen or three leaves of common carrots, and the animal will soon be all right.

When Cattle cannot make Water.

Take a good handful of parsley roots, and of the herb itself, cut fine, mix in water or wine, and give it to the cattle.

To make a Cow give a good supply of Milk.

When a cow, for the first time, calves, or while carrying a calf, give her half of the tail of an eel on a half slice of bread, and henceforth she will give milk in abundance.

To cause a Cow to become Pregnant.

Take nine knots of an earl tree in the spring of the year, pulverize them, and give to the cow upon newly baked bread.

For Rupture of any Animal.

On New Year's day thou shalt give to every cattle, laurel beans to eat before thou feedest them.

Remedy for Ulcer or Abscess of the Lungs. A Powder for the Cattle.

Take white (hawk-weed) wool herb, Veronica, Liver herbs, snake root, such as grows upon the trunks of oak trees, cross sage, ysops, wormwood, nasturtium, bay leaves, juniper berries, brown bethunia, lavender, both the leaves and flowers thereof, walnut tree ashes. Pulverize all these ingredients, and give weekly, a powder. In a very aggravated case, give one every two days, and when necessary, even twice a day, and thereupon give of the following preparation a wine-glassful.

An especially approved Powder for the Gravel.

Burn the blood of a hare and the entire skin in a new earthern pot to ashes, and give it to the patient dissolved in warm water. Let him take a spoonful before breakfast. It is astonishing what a powerful effect this powder exercises.

A certain Remedy against the protruding of Navels of Infants, also to prevent the Navel from growing too large.

Vegetable wax herb and the seeds thereof to be tied upon the child's navel, and the ailment will abate. Or, put a poultice made of shipspitch or rosin, and apply externally, which also is very efficacious.

A very good Recipe for the Colic.

Take a spoonful of olive or sweet oil, pounded crab eyes, and four carefully dried and pulverized peels of oranges, dissolved in good, warm wine. It relieves the pain immediately.

An Easy and Efficacious Remedy for the Dysentery.

The patient need only take a piece of the red mortar from a bake oven, as large as an egg, prepared as follows: Pound it in a mortar, and boil in river water, but take it cold. The ailment will cease almost instantly.

A certain Poor Woman's Good and Simple Remedy for the Worms.

This poor woman had a child which was afflicted by worms. She made use of the manure puddle, wherein she dipped a cloth, and laid the same frequently over the body of the child, and thus the child was freed from this terrible ailment.

When the Udder of a Cow is Bewitched.

Take blue bottle flowers, of which make a wreath; milk every stroke back of the legs three times upon the wreath; after this let the cow eat that wreath, and speak the following words: cow, I here give you bottle flowers that thou wouldst give me milk at once, that will not sour. Furthermore, whenever the cattle is driven out for the first time, in early spring, give to every piece of cattle a piece of beef meat about a half a finger long. This push down their throat after sprinkling it with a little salt. This will free them from becoming putrid and contracting erysipelas.

When a Cow does not Change herself.

Whenever a cow does not soon enough become purified after calving, give her hazelnut roots to eat.

To save the Cattle from Putrid Fever.

Cut a stick from an earl tree on Christmas night, put it in the manger, out of which the cattle feeds, and speak: I lay thee in the manger like Christ was laid into the manger at

Bethlehem, and that my cattle becomes as little putrid as Christ's body ever became putrid. † † †

In the spring time, drive the cattle the first time with that stick used on Christmas night; after that, save the stick in the manger, but change it again every Christmas night for a new one.

When Cattle are affected with Jaundice.

Take sponge (fungus) of an apple tree, old shoe soles and christianwort, also attic root, grind all to powder and give to the afflicted cattle, at night-time, a spoonful.

Secret Remedy of the great Theophrastus Paracelsus for Healing the Cancer.

This celebrated recipe is composed as follows: When a human being takes hold with his right hand of a live mole, and keeps the mole so long with a tight grip until it dies, such a hand obtains by dint of this miraculous proceeding, such marvelous power, that cancer boils, repeatedly rubbed, by moving up and down with this hand will break open, cease to form again, and entirely vanish.

A particular Performance by which it is caused that a Person will always obtain Right before a Court of Justice.

Take the herb called suntull (skunk cabbage) gathered during the month of August, while the sun stands in the sign of the lion, wrap a little thereof in a bay leaf, add a dandelion to it, carry this talisman on your person, and you will have the best of everybody, and receive the greatest advantage from it.

Another Trial to Detect a Thief.

When all the articles mentioned above are taken and laid upon the head, the person robbed may see the entire form and appearance of the thief.

Experiment made by a Mecklenburg Farmer, and by him related how to prevent any Dog from getting Mad.

This man said: Dogs should have scraped silver filings given to them upon a piece of bread and butter, Christmas eve, New Year's eve, and on the eve of Epiphany. Dogs thus treated will never become mad or rabid.

An Approved Remedy to prevent Horses from becoming Stiff.

Put, three Sundays in succession, before the rising of the sun, three handfuls of salt, and seventy-two juniper berries in the manger so that the horse will eat them, and wash the hind shanks with warm vinegar. Horses so treated will never become stiff nor stubborn.

A splendid and hitherto Secret Remedy for the Cure of the severest Pains caused by Gout to effect a Cure in fifteen Minutes.

After roasting a large and fine orange or lemon upon hot ashes, remove the peelings, pound them with anna Flor. Cassia in a glass mortar, and mix it with some breast milk to a poultice. This is an approved remedy and has relieved many persons.

A Remedy for the Fever by the Use of which an old Lady of Nobility has aided many People.

This matron of a noble family cut the ear of a cat, let three drops of the blood fall in some brandy, added a little pepper thereto, and gave it to the patient to drink.

An excellent Ointment for Old Sores on the Feet.

The following articles are necessary to make this ointment: one ounce of deer's tallow, two ounces of bees' wax, a like portion of white rosin, half ounce of white lead, three ounces of white bolus, six ounces of sweet oil, two ounces incense and mastic. The rosin and oil are left to boil together, and melt the wax therein, until it becomes stiff. After it has cooled off mix all the other articles to it; after they have been pounded, stir them well, and save up for use. Before applying this ointment to old sores, wash them first with warm sweet wine, then apply the ointment, and all will be well done to effect a result.

A Secret Remedy of much Efficacy for Gravel.

A hare caught in the month of March, you must burn, with skin and hair, until it becomes powder. Take bruised seed of parsley, add honey enough to make a syrup. Give to the patient early in the morning, before breakfast, and at night, before going to bed. The gravel will break, and cease for ever.

For Toothache and Neuralgia.

Write down, with a goose-quill and ink, new made—but be careful that nothing is wasted from the quill but what belongs to shape the pen—on the outside of the cheek, where the pain is situated, the following signs: "Mot, Tot, Fot." After this being done, light a candle, and proceed therewith under the chimney. Burn the pen by the light under the hearth, until not a vestige thereof remains. All this must be done noiselessly, while a person who suffers the pain must at once put the head in a bandage, retire to bed, and remain quiet, and by no means, speak a word to anybody for twenty-four hours.

When a Man or Cattle is Plagued by Goblins, or Ill-disposed People.

Go on Good Friday, or Golden Sunday, ere the sun rise in the East, to a hazlenut bush, cut a stick therefrom with a sympathetic weapon, by making three cuts above the hand toward the rise of the sun, in the name of the † † † Carry the stick noiselessly into the house, conceal it so that no one can get hold of it. When a man or beast is plagued by evil disposed people, walk three times around such a haunted person, while pronouncing the three holiest names; after this proceeding, take off thy hat and hit it with the stick and thus you smite the wicked being.

For Haunted Horses or Cattle.

Take the left-hand glove of a woman afflicted with rheumatism in the right arm, steep it in fresh water, and allow the animals to drink thereof.

For the Swelling of Cattle.

Give the cattle three roots of crowfoot flowers (ranunculus) to eat.

When we are perplexed to know what ails the Cattle.

Take half of an ounce of powdered alum mixed with salt, and give it to the cattle.

When Cattle has too much Gall.

Give it as soon as possible croton flowers to eat.

When a Person is Prevented from Passing Water.

Take a good handful of hare's hair, burn it till it becomes powder, wrap it in a handkerchief, add three handfuls of watercresses and a half a quart of wine, boil the powder and herbs therein. Drink it warm.

For Fresh Wounds.

Fresh is the wound, blessed is the day! happy the hour I found soon to stop and arrest thee, so that thou neither swell nor fester until mountains meet. † † †

For Arthritis or Pains in the Limbs.

Take two handfuls of fresh juniper berries, bruise them, boil them in a pint of old wine, add a glassful of brandy and put the whole in a cloth that is folded four times, and this apply to the place where the pain is located. It is an approved remedy.

For Sore Breasts.

Take distilled glori, five cents' worth; juniperberry salt, five cents; white beeswax, three cents; mercury precipitate, two cents; and let the mass be mixed in an earthen pot, on the fire until it becomes stiff like a salve. Stir it well, put some of it on linen, and apply once per day, upon the breast.

To Stay a Shot.

Shot stand still in the name of the Lord, give neither fire nor flame, as sure as the rock of Gibraltar remains firm. † † † While dissolving it, say: God saw his joy and glory!

To compel a Thief to return the Stolen Property.

Obtain a new earthen pot with a cover, draw water from the under current of a stream while calling out the three holiest names. Fill the vessel one-third, take the same to your home, set it upon the fire, take a piece of bread from the lower crust of a loaf, stick three pins into the bread, boil all in the vessel, add a few dew nettles. Then say: Thief, male or female, bring my stolen articles back, whether thou art boy or girl; thief, if thou art woman or man, I compel thee, in the name. † † †

Remedy to Remove the Secundines of a Cow.

Take bay leaves for three cents, boil them in a pint of wine vinegar, take it from the fire, cool it, then let a hen's egg remain in the fluid over night. After this steam the vinegar from the egg and bay leaves, mix the egg with the vinegar, and give it to the cow for a drink. Should it not be efficient, dry the bay leaves, powder and boil them again in a pint of vinegar. Let the mass stand over night and pour it into the cows, adding the powdered bay leaves.

To make a Magnetic Compass which will serve to Discover the Treasures and Ores in the Bowels of the Earth.

For this purpose a magnet made of the plusquam perfection, accompanied by the prime material of which all metals grow is requisite: with this, the magnet of the compass must be strengthened. Around the compass are engraved the characteristic signs of all the seven metals. If it is desired now to ascertain what kind of a metal is most likely to be found in a hidden treasure or in ore beneath the earth, it will be only necessary to hie to that particular spot, where the magnetic rod has given the indication, but you must put your foot there where the perpendicular shows its attractions, and take of every metal a small piece, that is, one as heavy as the other, and lay it upon the resp. character and the needle will rotate to that metal which predominates under the surface of the earth, and there it will stand still.

A Secret and curious Piece of Marvel, to Discern in a Mirror what an Enemy designs at the Distance of Three Miles or more.

Obtain a good plain looking glass, as large as you please, and have it framed on three sides only; upon the left side it should be left open. Such a glass must be held toward the direction where the enemy is existing and you will be able to discern all his markings, manœuverings, his doings and workings. Was effectually used during the thirty years' war.

To Destroy Worms.

The cancer is healed by means of a plaster made of the yellow of an egg, enzian, Easter herbs and centifolium, all mixed up to a powder. This preparation apply often.

A Remedy hitherto Secret against Sloth and Slough, commonly called Sweeny.

Dig three burdock roots on a Friday before the sun rises cut off every one of these roots, three round slices, sew them in a cloth, bind them over the sweeny limb or member, and let it remain there from two to four days, repeat as before until the part affected stops to ooze matter. The roots may be green or dry, it is all the same, if you only take care to dig them on a Friday before sunrise. Has been sufficiently tried on man and beast.

To prevent Fire Arms from being Bewitched.

Take nine blades of straw from under a sow while she is nursing young pigs, therefrom put nine knots into the shaft and insert them between the two barrel loops, and such a gun cannot be bewitched.

Secret Remedy for Healing the Cancer.

At the waning of the moon, take, several mornings in succession, a spoonful of elder flower seed in sweet milk; or in case the moon is waning, give to a child, plagued by worms, a small teaspoonful of sweet oil, and when the last quarter of the moon appears, the third spoonful, and the entire stock of worms will be passed by the child.

Hysterics accompanied by Fainting.

Take the warts commonly growing on the shanks of steers, cut them fine, dry them in an iron pan over a glowing flame until they become yellowish, bruise them gently and give of this powder as much as the point of a table-knife will hold, in wine or other liquor, to the patient, who must keep herself warm.

Against Violent Headaches.

Iron herb hung around the neck, or the essence thereof sprinkled upon the brow and temples, will cure the most violent headaches.

Account of an Experienced Fortune Hunter, how Treasures beneath the Earth Rise and Fall.

If one is contemplating to dig up a treasure, he should above all other things know, whenever the treasure stands highest, to rise with the sun and return again with the sinking of the same. If the treasure happens to be hidden in an open field, the affair will soon be righted by digging around, crosswise, or undermining, so that the treasure can be reached from below, but one must not be tardy in constructing the posts or galleries in order to prop the treasure in time, because the digger might otherwise be buried underneath the falling heap. But, if it can be so conducted that the sun can shine crosswise under the treasure, it may be raised, since the goblins of the earth have no longer the power to remove the same.

Marvelous Performances of an Experienced Pigeon Fancier. To prevent Pigeons from deserting the Pigeon Coops or Dove Cots, also, that no Pigeon Hawk can catch them.

Let the pigeons be put into the cot on a Friday, pluck off two feathers from the right wing of every pigeon before they are left to fly into the coop. These feathers should be fastened by a tack in the coop, so to prevent them from falling or flying away from the coop, because as long as the feathers remain in the coop no pigeon will desert, and no hawk will catch them; but it must never be forgotten to put some stonewort or some chickweed into their drinking water.

A specific Piece of Art by which all Dangers of Conflagrations are Avoided from a Dwelling House.

Take in the evening or in the morning a black hen from its nest, cut its throat, throw it upon the ground, cut the stomach of the hen from out of the body, but nothing else, and be careful to leave everything else inside. After this proceeding try to obtain a piece of gold quartz. The piece must be large as a saucer. These two articles wrap up together; take an egg laid on Green Thursday, wrap the three pieces thus obtained up in bees'-wax and put all in an octagon pot of clay, cover the same tightly, and bury it under the housedoor sill. Such a house is protected from all dangers of fire, although the flames may surround it.

A useful Way to make Boots Waterproof.

Take four ounces of sweet olive oil, sixteen ounces of tallow, four ounces of turpentine, eight ounces of common lard, and four ounces of new yellow bees'-wax, mix together, and after drying the boots, no matter what kind of leather they may be, well dried and slowly warmed, grease them with this mixture thoroughly, and no water will penetrate through them, and the feet will remain dry therein.

To Fasten a Thief.

Mary toiled and bore the child, three angels were her nurses, the first is named Saint Michael, the other's name Saint Gabriel, the third is called St. Peter. Three thieves approach to steal the child of Mary; Mary spake: Saint Peter bind. Saint Peter said: I have bound it with iron fetters, with God's own hands, that they must stand like a stick, and look like a buck until they are able to count all the stars, all rain drops that fall into the ocean, all grains of sand fro and to. If they cannot do this they must stand like a stick, must ever look like a buck, till I may see them with my own eyes, and with my tongue can bid them to arise and order them to go without ado. Thus I forbid the thieves my own, my all, and make the thief repent and fall. † † † Give the thief three times three strokes, and bid him depart hence, in the name of the Lord.

For Violent Toothaches.

Take a new nail, pick with this the tooth till it bleeds, then take this nail and insert it in a place where neither sun or moon ever shines into, perhaps, in the rafters of the bin in a cellar, toward the rising of the sun; at the first stroke upon the nail call the name of him whom you design to help, and speak: Toothache fly away, by the second stroke: Toothache cease, pain allay! † † †

When a Splinter or Thorn is Sticking in the Leg.

Take a white garlic onion, cut it fine, take the same weight of pitch, render the pitch down and dissolve the onion therein until it becomes the thickness of a plaster, which must be put upon the sore spot, which will soon heal, and the thorn may be easily removed.

Eyewater which makes the Sight Clear, so that no Spectacles are needed.

Take some good brandy of nettles, one drachm of ginger, camphor, fishberry, herb and nasturtium, of each one drachm, of cloves one scruple, of rue toothwort, eyebalm so much as may be held between two fingers (one pinch). Bruise all these articles, and put into the brandy, and distill it in the sun, during the winter season twenty-four days in a warm room. Dip your finger therein and rub the eyelids therewith, morning and evenings, this will keep the eyes clear, and make them strong without the use of spectacles.

An Amulet against Cramp.

Take white root of rhubarb, pulverize the same, and fill with such powder a square pouch made of linen, about three thumbs in size. The patient should carry the pouch on a string around his neck that it will touch the bare skin in the neighborhood of the stomach.

For Costive People.

Take half of a scruple or veronica or speedwell. Probatum est!

Ointment for the Scurvy.

Take a glass of wine, a glass of brandy, unwashed butter, smear soap, white beeswax, salt, pepper, cloves and a little of sulphur flower.

A Secret Art to banish Chicken Lice.

Strew malaxis herbs upon the floor of the hen-house, let it remain eight days therein, then wash it all clean again and the lice will have vanished.

For Bad Hearing.

Take the oil with which the bells of churches are greased, and smear it behind the afflicted ears, and relief will not fail to come at once.

To make a Saddle which will Press no Horse.

When a saddle is lined underneath with the rough skin of young does or fawns such a saddle will press no horse.

Secret Remedy of an experienced Farrier for the Swelling of Horses.

Take a newly spun yarn from the staple or reel, boil the same, and tie it while hot upon the swellings of the horse, twice a day.

When a Person cannot pass Water.

Take some black carroway seed, light colored incense grains, and let these evaporate upon coals, and inhale the vapors. Approved remedy.

When Delivery is too Slow.

Obtain from your apothecary some ursula; drink, and take it according to directions.

After Accouchment.

Take linseed oil, hempseed oil, two ounces of each, and three or four yolks of eggs, stir well in a dish, smear upon a cloth, and lay it upon the abdomen. Most excellent.

For Consumptive Lungs.

Take the ashes of juniper twigs, dissolve them in vinegar, and give it to the cattle.

Against Milk Thieves.

Take twigs of the hazel poplar tree, put them over the entrance of the stable door where the cattle go in and out. In case the cow is about to calve, break oak leaves from a young clearing, and feed them with it.

For the Worm.

Take of serpentine-tree bark, and grind it to a powder, mix with rock salt, and rub the tongues and roof of the mouth of the cattle therewith.

For the Erysipelas of Cattle.

Take a scarlet red lozenge, cut it small, give it to the cattle upon bread to eat. Or, give three may flowers.

How to drive away Bed Bugs.

Fern leaves gathered between the last two days of the month of June, and put under the bed, will drive away the bed bugs sure.

To make One's Self Invisible.

You must obtain the ear of a black cat, boil it in the milk of a black cow, then make a thumb cover of it and wear it on the thumb, and no one will be able to see you.

How to be able to see in the Darkest Night.

Grease the eyes with the blood of a bat.

To make an Incombustible Oil.

Common oil mixed with a strong lye and distilled, and the uppermost essence skimmed therefrom. The latter is incombustible.

How to Kill Bed Bugs.

Take of wormwood and rue a handful of each, mix them with common oil, also enough water, so that both water and oil will cover the herbs; after this boil the mass so long until all the water evaporates, whereupon squeeze the herbs in a press to obtain all the oil possible, and add a like quantity of mutton tallow; with this saturate the bedsteads, and the bugs will die.

To banish Spiders, House Flies, Gnats or Mosquitoes from a House or Place.

Engrave the figure of a spider or fly upon a piece of copper or tin, in the centre, engrave from one to twenty to the sign of the fish rising over the horizon in the zodiac, and while engraving, pronounce these words: This is the image which drives away all flies or spiders, forever and ever. Afterward conceal the plate in the centre of the house or suspend it in the middle of the house, or conceal it in the wall, where no one can take it away. This burying in the ground or concealing, must be accomplished when prima facies taurus rises, and thus it will come to pass that in such a house, no fly, etc., shall be seen.

To Destroy Mice.

In such food as they may like, mix mercury, or burnt lead, or particles of iron, produced by forging or black hellebore.

How to Improve all sorts of Inferior Wines. A Recipe hitherto kept secret, but known a long time since to a certain Elector of Mayence.

Take some superior tartar, smelt the same in a large crucible, but the fire under it must be fanned by a bellows, until the tartar shows a blue flame, when a wire is inserted. This will usually happen within an hour and a half, then it must be poured out, and quickly pounded in a warm mortar, to the size of small shot and then put into a distilling apparatus, add slowly so much of alcohol to cover the tartar, three fingers in height, shake well together. Expose it for several days and nights to a gentle, warm temperature, but stir it three times every day, the apparatus, however, must be well corked up. After the alcohol has obtained a fine red color, the same will be drained off, and a like quantity of other alcohol poured in; hence this extraction is performed three times. After this, then, all the extracts are poured together, and distilled in an elambic to a liquid. But should it be noticed that the alcohol becomes water, cease at once, in order to avoid that spirit of vitriol (phlegm) becomes mixed with it. Of this spirit, about one-half pound is made to run through a large tube into a cask of new-made wine or most in such a manner, so as not too rapidly to fall into it, but gently run over the new wine like oil runs smoothly over water; but, to accomplish this result, the cask must not be entirely full by two fingers in height, to give the spirit a chance to play and flow gently over the surface of the wine. This done, the cask is covered, but not closed with a bung, until one day and one shall have passed; after that time fill up entirely to have it ferment, and the task will be accomplished.

Another excellent Way to make Inferior and Bad Wine very Good and Wholesome.

Rec. sal. tartari, three ounces, cremoris tartari, four ounces, dissolve the sal. tart. in rain water, put it in a glass vessel upon glowing ashes, let it remain so until it begins to show bubbles, then add the crem. tart. by putting half a spoonful in at a time, until it dissolves no longer. Then filter and preserve it. To mix some of this fluid to some spoiled wine will improve the latter greatly. Or this: Rec. sal tartari per deliquium twelve ounces, cremor, tartari four ounces, proceed therewith as set forth above, to add of this a few drops in a glass of wine acts very good.

A Secret and most Excellent Masterpiece, how to Draw off or Distill a very good and costly wine.

The cask in which the wine is kept must be very nicely cleansed and rinsed, then pulverize one ounce of cinnamon bark, one ounce of Spanish pepper, one quart of enizian, one ounce of cloves, one drachm of sulphur flower, and one ounce of sugar; mix all these powdered articles together in a bag of linen about a span long, then close the cask with a bung, and let it rest quiet for three weeks, when the wine will be found to be elegant.

To manufacture a Golden Ring, by which not only House and Home, but also Man and Beast are secured against all Misfortunes, Pestilential Epidemics and Diseases, and are secured against the Arts and Wiles of the Powers of the Devil.

May God direct and rule, that this hour, day and year and all the time may be as good and blessed as our dear Lord Jesus Christ; that grant God, the Father, and God the Son, and God the Holy Spirit. Amen.

May God, the Father, make a golden ring around this house, around this stable, around all men and beasts that belongeth thereto and goeth in and out of it; also around my fields and forests, yea, this very ring encircles our beloved Mary with her dear infant, Jesus Christ they protect, watch over, maintain, shelter, cover and defend all mankind, both male and female, small and large, young and old, as likewise, all cattle, oxen, steers, cows and calves, horses and foals, sheep, goats, beef-cattle, and swine, geese, ducks, chickens, pigeons, large and small, whatever is contained in this house and these stables and all that cometh in and goeth out; for all misfortunes, evil, colic wild fire, losses, epidemics, and other diseases; for all bad and heated blood; for all bad and malicious enemies and storms; for all evil hours, day and night; for all magic power of witchcraft, and the designs and powers of the devil and his infernal hosts, to be visible or invisible, or for all wicked people who contemplate to rob me, that they may not be able to carry or spoil aught, anything that these people and animals, young and old, large and small, nothing excepted, whatsoever belongeth to these premises and their surroundings, and goeth out and cometh in, from whence and hence that no loss may occur, nor any evil be done at home or abroad, in the field or in the woods, in the meadows and on the plains, in grass, wood or heath, whether it works or rests, sits, lays, runs, or stands, they shall all now for all time to come be included in this ring, and be secure and protected from bullet and sword, by the very holy blood-drops of the dear beloved infant, Jesus Christ, which he hath suffered and shed for us by his circumcision and upon the cross and thereby vouchsafed and sealed his love everlasting, for such, they, the magicians will find no herb which may open, break or move or pervert, because our dear Lord Jesus Christ, protects and defendeth such with his ever holy hands, and his supremely sacred five wounds, at all times, by day and by night, and at all hours, forever and ever eternally. In the name of God the Father, the Son and the Holy Spirit.

Three Fridays in succession, in the morning, this should be repeated three times over house and all the estates, and all that lives and dwells therein will be protected from all evil and harm.

For Rows and Fights.

In the name of God, I do begin, lame your hands and feet because you sin, God grant that I may come out best or never I'll find peace nor rest, the true Son, Master, Jesus Christ, died on the cross for all mankind. † † †

For the Colic.

Mother was troubled, mother toiled and labored, lay against that very wall, where God did send them all. In the name of God, the Son and the Holy Spirit.

For Cunning Thieves, may they be ever so sly. Pronounce this grace every morning three times, over all thy possessions, with devotion.

Our dear mother in a garden came. Three angels comforted her there. The first is named St. Michael; the other, St. Gabriel; the third, St. Peter. Then spake Peter to our beloved Mary: I saw three thieves enter there. They intend to steal thy dear child and kill it. But the beloved mother Mary said: Peter, bind; St. Peter, bind; and Peter bound them with iron bands, with God's own hands, and with his holy five wounds, for this be with Gabriel, upon this day and night, and this entire year, and forever and all times, my possessions bound. Whoever attempts to steal therefrom, must stand still, like a stick, and see like a brick, and must stand quiet. He must go upward, that he cannot depart from hence until I permit him to proceed from thence. With my own tongue I must tell him this. This is my order and Gabriel's will, which now, by day and night, and all the year, for all times to come, will utter to every thief, for them to repent. For this may God his blessing lend. God the Father, God the Son, and God the Holy Spirit. Amen.

To Protect the Body from the Dangers of all kinds of Weapons, Projectiles and Guns, Shafts, Lancets, Swords, Knives Rapiers, Daggers, and Hellebards.

Jesus, the true God and man, protect me, N. N., from all sorts of arms and weapons, be they of iron, steel, lead, or be they nails, knives or wood, whatever was made and grew since the birth of Christ, is now forged, or may yet be forged, at any future time, of whatever material. Jesus Christ, the true God and man, protect me, N. N., from murder and from cannon balls, from bullets and swords, from thunder and lightning, fire and water, chains and prison, from poison and sorcery, from mad dogs and from shedding of blood, and from sudden death. Save me, Lord God. Jesus, the true God and man, protect me, N. N., from all sorts of arms and weapons, and all those who desire to overpower me. Cause that all their might and strength to be lost, and be vain.

N. N., hold and aim your armament and sword or lancet

toward the cross of Christ and his sacred five wounds, in all my troubles, and at all times; and command all shot and firearms that they may fail to give fire; and all swords, spears, lancets, and hellebards, and other pointed instruments, that their edges may become as soft as the blood of Christ, who suffered on the cross. Jesus, protect N. N., wherever I may be, against all enemies, be they visible or invisible, secret or open. The eternal Godhead may save and protect me through the bitter sufferings, death and resurrection of Jesus Christ, and through his holy rose-colored blood, which he shed upon the cross. Jesus begotten at Nazareth, born in Bethlehem, died in Jerusalem, crucified and tortured; these are truthful words, which are written in this letter, that I may not be captured by any murderer, or any other man, be killed, whipped, wounded, nor be laid in fetters; let move away from me, or yield my will. Fly and vanish until I shall recall them, all enemies and all arms, weapons and armament, may they be called by whatever name. None will injure me. All their power be lost on me. Lead and iron projectiles, remain quiet in your armament, for the sake of the martyred Jesus Christ and his holy five wounds. In the name of the Father, the Son and the Holy Spirit.

In case a person has a tumor growing, or warts of any kind upon his body, he or she shall go to church and, when he notices two persons speaking to each other, he shall touch the humor or wart, and recite three times: What I see is a great sin and shame, and what I touch may vanish soon.

When a couple of Oxen are to be trained, speak, while putting the yoke upon them, as follows:

Bless or Brown, take the yoke upon thee. Patient be, like Jesus Christ was patient. † † †

To Tame a Balky and Wild Horse.

Brown, Rap, Fox, or gray horse, be so tame and gentle, that whenever I sit upon thy back and ride thee, thou wilt bear me with as much patience as Jesus Christ was meek, patient, and humble. † † †

That Nobody may hurt you and how to be Secured against all Assailants.

Now I will walk over the threshold I met three men, not yet very old. The first was God the Father, the other was God the Son; the third was God the Holy Spirit. They protect my body and soul, blood and flesh, that in no well I fall, that water may not swell me at all, that a rabid dog may never bite me, that shot and stone may never smite me, that spear and knife may never cut me; that never a thief may steal the least from me. Then it shall become like our dear Saviour's sweat. Whoever is stronger and mightier than these three men, he may come hither, assail me if he can, or forever keep his peace with me. † † †

Powerful Prayer, whereby one may Protect Himself against Bullet and Sword, against Visible and Invisible Enemies, or all Possible Evil and Dangers

Count Philip of Flanders had a subject who had forfeited his life; and as the Count wanted to have the delinquent executed, no executioner was able to perform the act. No sword would cut his head off. This astonished the count, and he spoke thus: How shall I divine this? Tell me how this comes to pass, and I will pardon thee Whereupon the poor sinner showed him the letter, and he copied the same, as did all his servants. If you have to go to obtain advice, or to a court of justice, take this letter upon your right side, and you will not be subdued or conquered by any one. When you do not have the favor of your husband or of your wife, take this letter to your aid, and the favor will soon be regained When a woman is in her trouble hang this letter on her neck and she will bear with much patience. If one's nose is bleeding, and will not cease, put this letter upon such person's head—the blood will soon be stopped. Wherever this letter is put under the roof of a house, such property is secure from storm and lightning.

"The blood of Jesus Christ, who was God and man in one person, protect me, N. N., from all sorts of weapons and arms, projectiles and guns, long and short swords, knives, daggers, carbines, hellebardes, and all sharp, cutting and pointed weapons; from lancets and spears, short or long rifles, muskets, etc., wrought and forged since the birth of Christ, of all kinds of metal, be they of steel or iron, brass or lead, metal or wood. Jesus Christ, the true Lamb of God, save me, N. N., from all kinds of shot guns and projectiles, by maintaining the covenant, like the Holy Mary, before and after the miraculous birth, render their weapons to become as soft as the drops of blood shed by our Saviour upon Mount Olivet. Jesus Christ, protect me, N. N., from all evil reports behind my back; from apoplexy, sudden death, witchcraft, drying and stopping of well water; from all kinds of enemies, visible and invisible. Lord Jesus Christ, let me, N. N., not be lost but wander with me, and be with me, until my last moments, and leave me not, that I may not die here. That vouchsafe me, God the Father, God the Son, and God the Holy Spirit. Amen.

The Holy Trinity be with me and by me. It protect me, N. N., the one Godhead. Jesus Christ, be with me upon the water and upon the land; in the forest, mountains or valley; in village, town and city; wheresoever I stand or walk, sit or lay, or whither I roam. Lord Jesus Christ, save me, N. N., from all enemies, be they visible or invisible, secret or open. It protect me, N. N., the one God, through his bitter sufferings and death, and by his rose-colored blood, which the Lord Jesus Christ shed upon the Cross. Jesus Christ was conceived in Nazareth, born in Bethlehem. These are valuable and dear words, written down in this letter. Therefore all must succumb to me, N. N., that is, vanish until I recall them; and must loose all their arms and armor, defence and weapon, that they may give way and yield and vanish, until I call them again, and lose all their strength and power, like Pharaoh lost his might. Blood and strength retain your powers, like Christ retained his, when he was tortured, and with his Holy five wounds ye shall be nailed down and bound. The armament must vanish, like those men vanished who tied the hands of Lord Jesus upon the cross, in the name of the Father, the Son and the Holy Spirit. Jesus crossed the Red Sea, looked into the Holy Land, and said: Torn shall be all ropes and bands; all arms and weapons shall be broken; all eyes must be blinded, those that are sinful; no hero or any weapon shall overpower me. That water shall not cut—be it iron or steel, brass or lead, nor whatever it may be—must not hurt me, ah! God. May it be blessed, like the cup and the bread, like the real bread of life, which the Lord gave to His twelve disciples, in the name of God the Father, the Son and the Holy Ghost. The blessing of the Divine Being, how He blessed Lot, when he sent to make peace, may come over me; the blessing of the Lord when he blessed Joseph, it come over me. N. N.; the blessing of thy Lord over the archangel Gabriel, when he carried the joyful message to the Virgin Mary, it may come over me, N. N. In the name of God the Father, the Son and the Holy Ghost.

In the beginning was the Word, and the word was with God, and the Word was God. All things were made by him; and without him was not anything made that was made. In him was life; and the life was the light of men. And the light shineth in darkness; and the darkness comprehendeth it not. There was a man sent from God whose name was John. The same came for a witness, to bear witness of the Light that all men through him might believe. He was not that Light, but was sent to bear witness of that Light. That was the true Light, which lighteth every man that cometh into the world. He was in the world, and the world was made by him, and the world knew him not. He came unto his own, and his own received him not. But as many as received him, to them gave he power to become the Sons of God, even to them that believe on his name: Which were born, not of blood nor of the will of the flesh, nor of the will of man, but of God. And the Word was made flesh, and dwelt among us (and we beheld his glory, the glory as of the only begotten of the Father), full of grace and truth, visibly and openly protect me, N. N., the eternal Godhead, by the bitter sufferings and death, and through his rose-colored blood, which he shed from the Holy Cross. Jesus was begotten at Nazareth.

These are truthful words, as very stone is written down in this letter, that I will not be captured by any murderer, nor bound in fetters; all shots, arms and weapons will vanish before me, N. N., and lose all their power. Keep all thy armor and weapons, by the Almighty, in the name of God the Father, and the Son, and the Holy Spirit. Jesus walked over the Red Sea. He looked into the Holy Land. All cords and bands must break and bend; the eyes of my foes shall become blinded. Protect me, N. N., that no stone shall fall, nor iron, nor steel, metal or lead that I may be well blessed, like the very heavenly bread which the Saviour gave to the twelve disciples, in the name of God the Father, the Son, and the Holy Spirit. The blessing God bestowed upon the first created being may be inherited by me, N. N. Further: love my right hand, when I come into a strange land, that neither foe nor sorcerer may bewitch nor stun me. † † †

For the Epilepsy and Palsy.

Willow tree, I now beseech thee, I pray thee take away from me my seventy and seventy times epilepsy. This must be spoken three times, three Fridays in succession, when the moon is waning; mornings, before sunrise, go to a running water, and direct the face in the direction whence the water runs, and upon three willow barks make three knots in the name of the holiest being,

ss. sytz X X Z.

X E. S. X IL A. G. M. U. A. H. O. N. C. S. H. ss. H. Ghost.

Jesus of Nazareth, Jesus beware the words of God as to the blessing over the archangel Gabriel.

For a Ruptured Child.

When a child is afflicted with rupture, grease it with lard from a fox, and the rupture will soon heal.

When a Cow gives Blood in the Milk.

Take cowlip herbs and feed it to the cow, also boil these herbs in water and wash the udder with it; afterward, milk the cow over a glowing fire and let the smoke envelope the udder.

For Gout and Palsy.

God greet thee and take thee away, cold face I banish thee this day in the name of God and the last judgment day, go away and leave this marrow and bone, vanish from this flesh and blood, and I will praise our Lord and God.

A particular Way to recover Stolen Goods.

Mark well whence the thief left and by which door; from it cut three pieces of wood while pronouncing the three most sacred names, take these scraps of wood to a wagon, but in a noiseless manner, take a wheel off the wagon and insert the wood in the nave, again pronouncing the three holiest names, then drive the wheel backward and ejaculate: Thief, thief, return with the stolen article, thou shalt be compelled by the omniscience of God the Father, the Son and the Holy Spirit. God the Father calls thee back, God the Son turn thy footsteps that thou must return, God the Holy Spirit guide thee to retrace thy steps until thou again reachest this place. By dint of God's power thou must come back, by the wisdom of the Son of God thou shalt enjoy no peace nor rest till all the stolen things are returned to the rightful owner. By the grace of God the Holy Ghost, thou must run and leap, canst neither rest nor sleep till thou shalt arrive at that place where thou has committed the theft. God the Father bind thee, God the Son compel thee, God the Holy Ghost cause thee to return. The wheel, thou must not rapidly turn, or the soles of his feet may blister and burn, he will in pain and anguish cry, and ere you catch him, thus may die; Thou shalt come in the name of the Father, the Son and the Holy Spirit. Thief, thou must come. † † † Thief thou must come. † † † If thou art mightier, thief, thief, thief, than God and the Holy Trinity, then stay where thou art. The ten commandments force thee to observe not to steal, hence thou must return. † † † Amen.

When the Milk leaves the Cows.

Take camphor, eggs and black carraway seed, give it to the cattle, it does them good.

For the Lung Rot of Cattle.

Take orris root, cardamon root, boil in two quarts of wine and nine pints of water, till one pint has evaporated. Pour out one-half pint for the cattle to drink, mornings and evenings. † † † It is very good.

For Stitching Pains in Woman or Child.

Take goat's milk and a warm roll, and boil together, and apply the poultice as warm as possible upon the ailing spot and tie a towel around it. It will be cured.

To Drive away Swellings.

Take aniseed oil, turpentine oil, of each one-half an ounce, stir well and apply upon the swelling. It will soon improve.

To be enabled to shoot securely, upon the Stand, the Chase, or in the Field.

In the morning after rising, quietly say the following while taking the rifle in your hands: Rifle, I, N. N., take hold of thee in the name of God the Father, God the Son, and God the Holy Spirit, and accompany this grace by moving the palm of the hand over the barrel, continuing thus: That thou shalt be obedient to me, in all cases whatsoever, upon the stand, or for shooting wild game, thou shalt never fail, and wherever I wish to hit may surely hit, in the name † † † three times, and the following words inscribed upon the upper part of the barrel: Abia, Dabia, Fabia.

Ointment for a Boil that fails to Break.

Take some covidalis for five cents, a little honey, saffron, the yolk of an egg, and a little flour; put all of these articles into an earthen pot, mix well. This will give a most excellent plaster.

A Remedy to cure the Cough.

When cherries are in season, dry the stems of black cherries between two sheets of paper to prevent them from becoming dusty, save them in a paper box. Draw tea therefrom, for every drawing take about four saucers full of water, and as many cherry stems as may be held between three fingers. Boil like any other tea, and continue to take this tea till the coughing ceases. The most violent cough may be cured by this remedy.

Another Remedy to cure a Cough.

Roast an onion, rub the soles of the feet therewith, and the ailment will cease; or take strong brandy, dip a soft cloth therein and wet the soles of the feet, mornings and evenings.

For Sores on any part of the Body, whether caused by Pounding or Cutting especially when Erysipelas follows.

Take five cents' worth of saffron, very little of white lead, and two spoonfuls of goat's milk, make an ointment thereof, apply with a rag to the sore spot.

A Sympathetic Remedy for Fever.

Walk to a nut tree before sunrise, cut therefrom a piece lengthwise, write your name upon a paper, and put it in the empty space made by the cut, and speak: Nut tree I come unto thee, take the seventy-seven different fevers from me, I will persist therein in the name of God, etc., and while pronouncing this, place the cutling in its place again, that it may grow again together. It helps at once.

For Pain in the Back.

Buy five cents' worth of old sweet oil, same quantity of vobolium, sperm oil, baiberry oil—mix these four articles together, and grease the back therewith.

For Colic.

Take a few bay leaves and soak them in brandy in a warm room. As soon as the colic is felt, take from one to four spoonfuls of this remedy.

To cure Frosted Feet.

Take a white woolen cloth which has never been used before, burn it to ashes, strew these ashes upon the afflicted feet and they will heal.

To strengthen the Procreative Organs.

Take twelve ounces of imperial spices, two pounds of white sugar, twenty-four grains of opium, one ounce of borax, four ounces prepared steel filings, twenty drops of cinnamon oil, twenty drops of oil of cloves; of these articles prepare a powder. Take a pinch, or as much as covers the point of a table knife, every hour throughout the day. Bathe the body often in warm water, and the organs in cold water. After this cure you will be stronger than ever before.

To drive away Vine Fretters and Wall Lice.

Take four ounces of arsenic, two ounces of antimonium, eleven and one half ounces of mercury, one quart of hog's lard, which must be rendered in turpentine; of these ingredients make an ointment, and smear the places therewith, wherever these insects prevail.

For Intestine Colic of Horses.

Move your hand three times over the back of the horse, and speak, Oh! Jerusalem, thou city of the Jews, wherein Christ hath been crucified, where he changed into water and blood, this shall be good for horses warm, colic and fefes, in the name. † † † Whatever is troubling thee, all shall be healed. † † † Whenever you say this grace, always tap the left side, and it will be more efficacious.

When Cattle is affected by Knots.

Mix some leaven, or yeast, and apply to his throat.

When a Horse has the Fifes, or Vifes, or Worms.

Throw his water into the left shoe, and then pour a little of the water into the right ear, and the horse will be cured.

For White Swelling, and Joint Water.

Hogs manure and a little excrementis hippo, put in a left shoe and tie over the afflicted spot, and it will cease.

When the Limb of a Horse becomes Less or Decays.

Take common nettles and rub the member or limb therewith, afterward take crabs alive, pound them so that they pass water, and with such water wash the animal.

When a Person is Cut or Pounded.

Speak thus: Wholesome is the wound, wholesome is the hour and sound, that this may not swell or fester again until the seas run dry.

For Suppuration of Man or Beast.

Take a field toad which, during harvest time, had been put upon a stick, and placed in a position toward the rising sun where it died. Of such a toad take the corresponding limb of that part of which the patient suffers, be it man or beast, and tie it to the ailing limb.

To Secure One's Self against Wicked People whilst Traveling, and being in Danger of being Attacked.

Speak three times: Two wicked eyes have overshadowed me, but three other eyes are overshadowing me too, the one of God, the Father, the other of God the Son, the third of God the Holy Spirit, they watch my blood and flesh, my marrow and bone, and all other large and small limbs, they shall be protected in the name of God. † † †

When a Horse has Swelled Legs.

Take bark of white-horned shrub and some cones of a fir tree, boil in lye, and wash the limbs therewith.

For a Putrid Mouth.

Take blackberry leaves boiled in water and wine, put a little alum to it. The mouth rinsed therewith, will have a good effect.

For Gravel.

Take hurbum oviga aurea, grind to powder, give the patient every morning a spoonful in an egg, and let him fast afterward four hours. The patient will urinate an hour thereafter, and after using this remedy for about ten or twelve days, all the gravel in his kidneys will break, and he will pass them without suffering any pain.

For the Colic of Infants.

Hast thou heartburn and colic? Leave this rib, N. N., like Jesus Christ left his manger. † † † Three times repeated. The two N. N. signify the name of him who is to be comforted.

Now I step out in God's great name, now step out in his might and fame, now I step out in God's footstep right which is against all spirits' might. God, the Father before me is, God, the Son behind me and at my side, God, the Holy Spirit is within and with me. † † † Speak three times and move with the hand over the sore.

For a Plaster.

Take olive or sweet oil, camphor, red lead, five cents' worth of each, and prepare into an ointment.

For the Toothache.

Write upon a piece of paper, Quosum sinioba zenni tantus lect veri, and hang it on a string over the back.

For the Goitre.

Take goitre fungus and burn it to a powder over a coal fire or alcohol flame. Take of this powder mornings and evenings, on an empty stomach; as much as two five cent pieces will cover.

To Heal the Hernia or Rupture.

Write the name of the patient upon paper, drill a hole in three prune trees, and prepare an oaken bolt, and put into every hole the three most sacred names, drive every one of these bolts in with three strokes, and pronounce the following sentence; N. N., I drive your rupture into this tree, God may thy physician be; Rupture forget thy growth and walk, like our Lord forget one man; hernia leave my flesh and bone. Rupture, rupture, rupture, depart hence in the name of the Lord, etc. I beseech thee in the name of the living God, that thou may heal upon the rod, that thou may become sound and straight, and growest stronger every day. Hepheta open thyself! † † † A. O. B. Tibas.

To prevent that the Fire on the Hearth becomes extinguished.

When a new house is built, write upon three separate pieces of paper: Deus Pater, Deus Filius, Deus Spiritus Sanctus in Oleum Trinitatis Sun and Moon have their course over water and over land, that no fire and flame in this house shall cease. above inscriptions be placed, and on three corners under the For this, three tin boxes must be made, and in each one the threshold or stones be laid, so that they do not decay or moulder in the ground, and the fires in such a house will never go out.

When Cattle is Afflicted with Warts, Tumors, etc.

Anna Important, Anna Jesus Christ, break spontaneous growth and blister wherever thou art; cattle is plagued by tumor and warts, in mouth and on the head, in the throat, or on the glands, in blood, in flesh, depart from hence, into the lake over the fence, but not into the flesh. † † † Press the yoke of an egg into the throat of the animal, in the name. † † †

How to cure a Boil or Swelling on the Face.

Procure five cents' worth of melioration plaster, (easy plaster,) put it on the boil before going to bed. Another most excellent remedy is Unguentum Balsilicon.

To prevent Persons doing Evil unto you, whom you suspect of bearing Malice, or designing Evil against you.

Welcome, in the name of God, ye brethren true and God, we all have drank of the Saviour's blood. God the Father be with me; God the Son be with you; God the Holy Spirit be with us all. Let us meet in union and part from each other in peace. † † † Three times spoken.

A good Plaster for Open Sores.

Take five cents' worth of bees-wax, the same quantity of ropemakers' resin, some few ounces of beef suet, a few teaspoonfuls of sweet oil, that is, the same quantity in weight of each of the ingredients, boil over a quick fire to the substance of a salve, and use like a plaster.

For Fevers.

Write upon three almond kernels the following words, and take them three mornings in succession:

"HASTA, HAVA, SHAVER."

Then purchase five cents' worth of camphor, and make small lozenges from it, and suspend these from your neck. Leave them three days and three nights in that position, and remove them at the same hour of the day that they were fastened to your body.

To Extirpate Rats and Mice.

Take fine iron or steel filings. Mix the same with ground willow wood into a dough. If this dough is put into the mouse holes, the mice will be eager to devour it, and soon die.

2. Take leaves of white hellebore, mixed with fine wheat flour, and knead into a stiff dough, with honey. This dough put into the holes when the rats and mice run in and out. They will eagerly devour, and surely die.

3. Or, take bitter almonds and fine wheat flour, make a stiff dough, and dispose of it as already stated.

4. Take potassa, and strew into the mouse and rat holes. This sometimes kills the entire brood in a few hours.

5. Take Halesia seed, and throw it into the holes. This they eat with greediness, and certain death will follow.

6. Take the rinds of wild gourds or pumpkins. Mix the same with equal portions of wolf's wort (Chrysanthemum) and barley flour. Of these articles make a stiff dough. Rats and mice eating of this will meet sure death.

7. Take the head of a rat or mouse, draw the skin therefrom, and put the head in the place where these vermin congregate, and they will fly at once in great haste, as if they were bewitched, and never more return for fear that it might be done unto them as to their dead kindred.

8. Another good exterminator is to take the herb skunk cabbage, symplocarpus fœtidus angustifolium, and fumigate the place infested with the mice. As long as this odor touches their nostrils they will stay away.

When a Cow loses the Milk.

Inscribe the following words upon an iron spade: Mura, Martha, Marscha, T. X. T. Make a spade red hot, dip into the milk of such a cow three times, and three Fridays in succession repeat this. It is magnificent.

For Griping Pains or Colic.

The mother of God journeyed over the land, when the Saviour met her with His band. The Saviour spoke thus; Whither art thou going? The Virgin Mary replied: I will plague mankind. The Saviour said: Nay, thou shalt not do so. † † † Three times, and with the thumb move around the body.

To prevent lameness, when the veins are cut or torn.

Take cart worms, pound them in old grease, and tie this

EGYPTIAN SECRETS.

tepid mass over the wounds, and on the fourth day thereafter the veins will have healed together, and without pain.

To cause the Hair to Grow wherever you wish.

Take milk of a slut, and saturate therewith the spot wherever the hair is desired to grow. Probatum est!

To Ascertain whether a Sick Person will become well again.

Cut a piece of bread, rub the patient's teeth therewith, and throw it before a dog. If he eats it, the patient will recover. Otherwise, the disease is dangerous.

To Prevent from being Wounded.

Whoever digs up St. Peter's root in the morning of St. Peter's day, before the sun rises, and carries these roots around the neck, is sure not to be wounded. But such a person must be careful not to drink liquor while carrying the roots.

Also, whoever digs knot grass, on St. John's day, in the morning before sunrise, and carries the same, will not be wounded.

Another Preventive for the Same.

Dig meadow rue in the sign of the zodiac virgo, eat them before breakfast, before beginning to fight or battle. Probatum est.

To Drive away Lice and Nits from the Head.

To drink powder of hartshorn dissolved in wine, prevents the growing of these vermin on the head. If such powder is strewn upon the head, all lice and nits will surely die.

For Gravel, a Simple and Effective Art.

This herb boiled in beer, and drank mornings and evenings, is a miraculous remedy.

How to draw the Poison from a Body.

Drink four ounces of rosemary water, it will neutalize the poison and stengthen heart and brain.

A Good Salve for Itchy Hands.

Take meadow rue, boil in olive oil, mix a little bees-wax

therewith, so that it becomes a salve. Grease the hands with it, and soon they will be all well.

To Restore Manhood.

Buy a pike as they are sold in the fish-market, carry it noiselessly to a running water, there let whale oil run into the snout of the fish, throw the fish into the running water, and then walk stream upward, and you will recover your strength and former powers.

Another Remedy for the Above.

Take a new fresh laid egg, if possible, one that is yet warm. Pour whale oil over it, and boil the egg in it; the oil then should be poured into a running water, stream downward, never upward, then open the egg a little, carry it to an ant's hill, of the large red specie, as are found in fir-trees forest, and there bury the egg. As soon as the ants have devoured the egg, the weak and troubled person will be restored to former strength and vigor.

Remedy for the Hydrophobia.

The "Swabian Mercury," a German daily, printed at Stuttgart, Germany, contains in No. 181, Monday, September 10, 1810, the following article, with regard to hydrophobia, which deserves to be reproduced and embodied into this book:

"The County-Physician, Dr. Schaller, in Baireuth, has recently performed a very successful cure, at the country-seat of the Master of the Royal Forest, Baron de Hardenberg in Karolinenreuth. The doctor has successfully restored to her wonted health a four-year-old girl, who was bitten by a mad dog, despite all the symptoms of hydrophobia, having already been developed, by the application of belladonna and water of distilled laurel-berries. Thus it was proven that there is really a remedy for this terrible malady, even after it has taken hold of the unfortunate victim.

A similar power is ascribed to aniseed oil, if several drops thereof, poured into the wounds, made by the biting of the rabid animal, or of any other poisonous animal or bird. The oil put on a cloth, and laid upon the wound, will draw the poison therefrom, and leave no injurious effects.

To Clarify Wine.

Take a half nutmeg, two ounces of cinnamon bark, two ounces of cloves, four ounces of white sugar, one dram of cream of tartar, then take white sugar, and render down in an earthen pot; this done, take a glass of water pour it into the pot after the sugar dissolves, and take the pot from the fire, then add a pint of wine, stir all, and pour the mixture into the cask. Repeat this procedure several times, let the wine settle for an hour, and after this the wine will be as clear and fine as good old wine.

An approved Method to turn Conflagrations and Epidemics to Usefulness.

The following is the invention of a Gypsy King of Egypt, who confessed Christianity. Anno 1714, on the 10th day of June, there were executed, in the kingdom of Prussia, six gypsies, by suffering death on the gallows; the seventh of them, however, who was a man of eighty years, was condemned to be beheaded on the 16th of the same month. But a conflagration taking place, meantime, turned to good luck for the aged man. He was liberated, and taken to the scene of the fire, for the purpose of having him try his arts and mysterious workings. What he accomplished, to the great astonishment of all present, he stayed the conflagration, by a miracle, within the brief period of a quarter of an hour; and, for this deed, he was pardoned, and entirely liberated. Such was approved by the royal President, Government and the Superintendent General at Kœnigsberg, and made public in print.

First: printed at Kœnigsberg, Prussia, by Alexander Bauman, Anno 1715.

Thou art welcome, thou fiery guest, do not grasp further, but spare the rest.

That fire I count to thy ransom, in the name of the Father, the Son, and the Holy Ghost.

I command thee, fire, by the power of God, that thou wouldst stand still, and not further proceed; as true as Christ stood on the river Jordan, when he was baptized by Holy St. John;

that I count to thy ransom, oh, fire, in the name of the Holy Trinity.

I command thee, fire, by the power of God, that thou wouldst allay thy flames, as true as Mary remaineth so chaste and pure; for this cease thy rage, oh, terrible fire. This I count to thee, oh, terrible fire, for ransom's sake, in the name of the Holy Trinity.

I command thee, fire, thou wouldst thy violent heat allay, for the sake of Christ's blood. Thy rage now stay, for the blood which he shed for our sins and his death. All this I accept as a ransom for thy sake, in the name of God the Father, the Son, and the Holy Ghost.

Jesus Nazarenus, King of the Jews, help us out of these dangers of fire, and protect this land and its borders from all epidemics and from pestilence.

Whoever keeps this letter in his house, he will not suffer from conflagrations; and if any parturient woman carries this letter upon her person, no sorcery, apparition or witchcraft can harm her. Also, every one who keeps this letter at home, or carries the same on his person, will be secure from dire epidemics and pestilence. † † †

Truthful Discovery by an Old and Celebrated Physician how to tell all Diseases by the Water.

1. That water which in the surface is lead colored or shows a lead colored circle around the muddy substance, indicates a clodded brain. Also, epilepsy and other troublesome condition of the head.

2. The water of a person who dies of apoplexy shows a green circle, with blueish bubbles therein, and the circle trembles.

3. A patient having a diseased head, passes water of a lead color. The circle on the surface is also greenish. This is a symptom of death.

4. A subtile froth of the water, with lead colored surface, indicates heat of the lungs, the heart, the breast, and of the liver, while a reddish water always proves a heated liver. Red gravel in the water, without fever and pains in the loins, signifies heat of the liver and kidneys. A cloudy, foaming water, of yellow-

ish and greenish hue, indicates great heat of the liver. Pure blood in the water, accompanied by pains and severe stitches in the right side, is a sure sign of blood in the liver. A reddish and cloudy water indicates bile in the liver, especially should the water be mixed with matter or pus, and has a very offensive odor. Water mixed with a red and blackish substance, indicates a greatly inflamed liver.

5. A red, thick water, and, when shaken, showing a saffron yellow color, indicates jaundice.

6. A thick, fattish and white water indicates consumption, while a cloudy, lead-colored water, when the clouds first appear on the bottom, forebodes consumption; and a pale water of a consumptive person is a certain sign of an early death.

7. If the fever is violent, a blackish water indicates violent headaches and loss of reason. A black water, at the breaking of a fever, which so remaineth until the seventh day, is a foreboding that the patient is recovering from fever. A black water in a fever, while the patient perspires on the head, neck and back, is a sign of early death. A water of greenish color, with a circle around it during a heavy fever, signifies head disease. Reddish, soft gravel in the water, during the prevalence of a fever, signifies a burnt fluid. A clayish, fatty water, during fevers, is a sign of consumption and marasmus.

8. If a man is attacked by a violet fever, the water will be very red, and much bad pus oozes out with it.

9. Irritation, painfulness, heat or difficulty in discharging water, may arise from a variety of causes; but by far the most common is the irritation produced by the presence of bile in the water caused by a deranged state of the liver.

10. A water containing a little matter, indicates boils of the kidneys. Red or yellowish curls in the water, show heat in the kidneys. Hair curls in the water, when they are coarse, and soon vanish when the trial glass is shaken, are a criterion of constipation and coarseness, and dingy mould of the kidneys.

11. When the water has become scaly and the patient complains of spasmodic pains in the abdomen, it is a sign of irregularity in the bowels, and originates from a diseased bladder. Water containing much pus or matter indicates a boil

in the bladder. White, hard water, having a bad odor, indicates a diseased bladder. Whitish and hard water, with a sediment on the bottom of the vessel, is a sure sign of gravel in the bladder.

How a Farmer may be enabled to Predict the Future State of the Weather during the Year, from the first day of January, or from the Days of the First Week in which the New Year's Day Comes.

If New-Year's Day falls upon a Sunday, a quiet and gloomy winter may be expected, followed by a stormy spring, a dry summer, and a rich vintage. When New-Year's Day comes on a Monday, a varied winter, good spring, dry summer, cloudy weather, and an inferior vintage may be expected. When New-Year's comes on a Wednesday, a hard, rough winter, a blustry, dreary spring, an agreeable summer, and a blessed vintage may be hoped for. If the first of the year happens to come on Thursday, a temperate winter, agreeable spring, a dry summer, and a very good vintage will follow. If on a Friday the year begins, a changeable, irregular winter, a fine spring, a dry and comfortable summer, and a rich harvest will be the result. If New-Year's Day comes on Saturday, a rough winter, bleak winds, a wet and dreary spring, and destruction of fruit will be the consequence.

How to Prevent Pigeons from Flying away or Staying away from the Coop.

Take a small board from a bier from which a small child was buried which died before baptism. Lay the board under the pigeon hole, and they will return again, provided they are not caged up, even if they should be carried many miles from their home. But if you desire that your pigeons bring strange pigeons along, you must give them mortar and lime from an old bake oven to eat, mix such lime with a little aniseed. They love to eat this, and while other pigeons smell the odor of yours, they will follow and fly with them to the coop.

When Milk is Stolen by Witchcraft.

Wash the outside of the milk pails which you use for milking with essence of Tonquin bean. Repeat this several times while milking the cows, and the witches' butter and cheese will have a bad odor, such as is frequently observed.

To Glue Broken Glass Together.

Take albumen, (white of eggs,) mix unslaked lime to it, and, with this glue, broken glass and earthen dishes may be mended.

An Excellent Recipe for Pestilence.

Take garlic and rue. Boil in good wine vinegar. Drink this mornings and evenings. It is a sure cure.

The Art of Extinguishing Fire without the aid of Water.

Inscribe the following letters upon each side of a plate, and throw it into the fire, and forthwith the fire will be extinguished:

```
S A T O R
A R E P O
T E N E T
O P E R A
R O T A S
```

For Epilepsy.

Purchase a half-grown black rooster. Capon the fowl. Take a nutmeg, and put it into the place from which you make the cut. Leave this nutmeg in its place until the rooster is fat. Then kill the fowl, withdraw the nutmeg, and scrape, evenings and mornings, the point of a knife full, and add it to a spoonful of soup, which is given to the patient. Furthermore, the baptismal name of the afflicted person must be written six times upon a piece of paper, and lay it under the head of a corpse. Furthermore, perspire in a linen cloth, and wrap around a dead person. If it is a female who has this disease add to the powder made by burning to a crisp a lock of her hair. In case of a male person, leech him, and dip a rag into blood, and let it be buried with the corpse. Probate.

How to make Yourself Bold and Amiable.

The stone called Actorius is to be found in the craw of any old capon. He who wears such a stone on his neck, will always remain bold and beloved by all mankind.

How to Manage in Selling Cattle you wish to Dispose of.

Drive through a running water, and pour three handfuls of water over the animal, and speak each time as follows:

Every one shall run after me to purchase my cattle from me. As true as Christ baptized with the water from the river Jordan, so I, too, baptize thee. † † †

To Vanquish a Man.

I, N. N., will breathe on thee, three drops of blood I draw from thee. The first from thy heart, the other from thy liver, the third from thy vigorous life. By this I take all thy strength, and thou losest the strife. † † † Three times.

Against Worms in the Body of a Man.

St. Peter and Jesus moved upon the acre. They dug up three furrows, where they found three worms. The one was white, the other is black, the third is red. Henceforth, N. N., all thy worms are dead. Three times.

A Blessing and Grace for all.

Jesus, I will arise. Jesus, do go with me. Jesus, put my heart into thine own bosom. Christ is ascended! Bliss hath invested him, woes that molested him, trials that tested him, gloriously ended. † † †

For the Toothache.

St. Peter stood under an oak tree. Then spake our beloved Redeemer to Peter: Why art thou sad and weary? Peter replied: Why should I not feel sad and dread, since all the teeth decay in my head. Whereupon our Lord Jesus Christ spake unto Peter! Peter, hie to the cool and lonely nook, there runs a clear water in a mountain brook. Take water thereof in thy decaying mouth, and spew it again into the running brook. † † † This done three times in succession, and each time the three highest names pronounced. This repeat for three days in succession.

To Stay a Shot.

Three drops of blood flowed over the holy face of our Lord. These three holy blood drops are moved before the touch-hole of the weapon, and remain as pure as the mother of God. No more shall fire and smoke from thy barrel and touch-hole go. Gun, let neither fire nor smoke from thy barrel move, nor heat. Now, I go thither, because God the Lord moves with me; God the Son accompanies me; God the Holy Ghost, he soars o'er me forever and ever, that bullet and sword will hurt me never. † † † Three times.

To Banish all Robbers, Murderers, and Foes.

God be with you, brethren. Desist you, thieves, robbers, murderers, waylayers, and warriors in meekness, because we all have partaken of the rose-colored blood of Jesus Christ. Your rifles, guns, and cannons be spiked, with the holy drops of our Redeemer's blood. All sabres and deadly weapons be closed, with the five wounds of our dear Master, Jesus Christ. Three roses are blooming on Jesus' heart. The first is kind, the other is mighty, the third represents God's strong will. Under these, ye thieves and murderers are become still, as long as I will, and ye are banished, and your foul deeds have vanished. † † †

To alleviate Pains.

Our dear Lord and Redeemer Christ suffered much boils and wounds but never had them tied and bound. They fester not, they pester not, neither do they ever suppurate. Jonas was blind, but the heavenly child was kind, and spake to him: As true as with the holy wounds thou art smitten, they will not curdle, nor ever fester; but from them I take water and blood, be it for N. N.'s pains and wounds ever good. Holy is the man who all sores and wounds can heal. † † †

When they shall be Released again, speak:

Change place, and sense ensnare: be free, be here and there! God perceiveth his joy and glory. † † †

A Good Way to Stay a Thief.

Three lilies grow upon Jesus' grave. The first is courage divine; the other, God's blood, so fine; the third is God's will, under which, ye thieves, must hold still. Stand still you thief. No more our Lord Jesus descendeth from the cross. Thou shalt not be able to leave this spot. This I command thee, in the name of the four Evangelists and the heavenly elements in the waters or in the shot, in the court of justice or before an apparition. This I bow unto thee by the day of doom, that thou standest still, and not further proceed, till all the stars in the heaven I shall see and the sun will shine bright. I herewith stop all thy leaping and escaping. This, I command thee, in the name of God the Father, the Son and the Holy Ghost.

When you desire to set them free again, order them to depart hence, in the name of the Lord.

To Cause the Return of Stolen Goods.

Go early in the morning, ere the sun rises, to a juniper tree, and, at sunrise, bend it to the ground, and put a stone upon it. Under this stone and tree lay the skull of a criminal and speak: Juniper tree, I bend and press thee until the thief shall return N. N.'s stolen property to its place. † † † When the thief has returned the stolen booty, move the stone from whence you took it, and put the bush in its proper position.

To Restore the Usefulness of a Cow.

Write the words given below upon three scraps of paper, and nail one on the outside of the stable door, the other on the manger, and the third tie to the left horn of the cattle, and speak:

L. bian † punctum † sobat †
L. bian † punctum † sobat †
L. bian † punctum † sobat †

This assault and trouble shall cause thee no more pain, as it be to our dear Lord in heaven and all his disciples, as little as God the Father, as little as God the Son, as little as God the Holy Ghost. † † †

Whenever Cattle are Troubled with the Diarrhœa.

Take a good handful of lintels, boil them in water till they become stiff, and feed the cattle with this. Cheese may also be applied.

To Cut a Stick wherewith to Punish a Witch that has Attacked the Cattle.

Mark well, and observe when the new moon shines on a Tuesday before sunrise, or, perhaps, on a Golden Sunday, which will occur whenever a Friday and Sunday come together, or, perhaps, on Good Friday, also before the rising of the sun, hie thee to a hazelnut bush, which you may have selected beforehand. Stand before the stick toward the rising of the sun, take hold thereof, in the name of God, with both hands, and speak: Stick, I grasp thee, in the name of God the Father, the Son, and the Holy Spirit, that thou shalt be obedient to me, that I may surely hit him whom I design to whip. Whereupon take thy knife, and cut the stick in three cuts, while pronouncing the three highest names, and carry it quietly to thy home, and guard it well, that no person steals it. If you intend to whip a witch which hath assaulted a beast or human being, go into the resp. house, and pray, before proceeding thence, three times, with great devotion, the article dedicated to the Bedgoblin, (which is the second article in this book), so that she may be destroyed by fire, and no evil spirit may enter into house or stable; otherwise the cats would get madam to scratch the eyes out of your head. Then move round the man or beast so bewitched three times, backward. Now take off the hat, put it upon the floor, and batter so long upon the hat as thou may chose. It will certainly hit the witch; and even if you should hammer holes into your hat, even the witch will then receive holes in his (or her) head. If thou desirest to flog one who is living at a distance from you, who deserves a beating, then place your coat upon a witch's ladder or shears, or upon a threshold, and call the name of him (or her) you design to whip, and you will hit him (or her) just as well as if he (or she) be present. But upon the stick thou must inscribe: Abiam, Dabiam, Fabiam. Probatum est!

For the Fever.

Suspend, upon a Friday, a letter containing the names set forth below, between the hours of eight and nine, upon the patient's neck, in the following manner:

Fold together, and tie it in grayish red cloth, which must be unbleached, and pierce through the cloth and the letter, three holes. Draw red thread through them, while calling the three holiest names. Suspend the same around the neck of the patient, and let it remain eleven days. After taking it off, burn it before the lapse of one hour:

```
H B R H C H T H B R H
H B R H C H T H B R
H B R H C H T H B
H B G H C H T H B
H B R H C H T H
H B R H C H T
H B R H C H
H B R H C
H B R H
H B R
H B
H
```

For a Toothache.

Take a new, but useless nail. Pick the teeth well with it, till they are bleeding. Then take the nail, and drive it into a rafter, toward the rising sun, where neither sun nor moon shines, and speak, at the first stroke, Toothache, vanish; at the second stroke, Toothache, banish; at the third stroke, Toothache, thither fly.

When a Beast has the Erysipelas, and the Water looks as Red as Blood.

Write the letters below upon a hen's egg, and give it the animal to eat:

† K a o r K S S O r E z o n r h
a r K O C tz tz a h u r o x K a o tz a
E a E S x i i x a r o t t t o x

To Protect Cattle against the Rot.

Stew some juniperberry ashes in vinegar, and give it to the afflicted cattle. It stops the rot.

For the Goblins and Puppets who deprive the Cows of their Milk.

The appended formula, written upon a scrap of paper, and nailed in a secluded spot in a stable.

† Janna † Sarult † Dutter † Jer † or
† Janna † Sarult † Dutter † Jer † or
† Janna † Sarult † Dutter † Jer † or

For Spots and Cataracts on the Eyes.

When man or beast is hit in the eye, so that a skin grows over the eye, suspend the following words from the neck of such a person or beast: GAA, SAGA, FASSAA.

For Griping Pains and Colic.

Grips and colic, I bless thee on this holy day, that thou wilt get from my cattle and horses away. † † † Three times recited. Afterward take a spoonful of chimney soot, another handful of ashes from juniper wood, half a quart of old wine, and give all at once to the animals.

To Cause a Cow to Give a Good Supply of Milk.

During Christmas night take the milt of a herring, and the sinew thereof; also, bay leaves, saffron, black carraway seed, and mix together; spread upon four pieces of bread, and give it to the cow.

A Drink for Sick Cattle.

Take vinum crecum, enzian, alum, sulphur, mesturtian roots, angelicum of Indian cucumbers, (medeola,) steep it and give it to the cattle, but warm.

For Pulmonary Diseases, Consumption, Jaundice and Black Disease.

Purchase fifteen cents' worth of aniseed oil. An aged person may take twice per day, in the morning before breakfast, and evening before retiring to bed, twelve drops in a spoonful of brandy. If he feels improvement, continue thus till no more slime passes, then cease to take this drink. Many a person suffering from diseased lungs and jaundice have been cured thoroughly by this most excellent and simple remedy. For young men and females it is not of any use; except for barren women, in such a case it may be taken from three to four days, but during this time abstain from all excitement, otherwise it will be of no use.

A certain Art to kill Flies.

Take sweet milk, add black pepper to it, mix well, and leave it for the flies to eat. All flies that partake of it will die.

When a Man Loses his Speech or the Tonsils Fall.

If the speech is impeded or the tonsils swollen, grease the centre of the head with grease from a stork, and the power of speech will return.

How the Oil of Earth Worms are Made, and what Good Use is made thereof.

It serves in cases of anthritis or neuralgia as well as for the withering of limbs and warts on hands and feet, corns on feet, heels, ruptures, and other injuries of all kinds. Put the earth worms into a pot and wrap the same up in a loaf of bread, bake it in a bake oven as long as is necessary for bread to bake, then put it in a glass vessel, and distil in the sun.

The Usefulness of Black Snails.

They cure withered limbs and warts on hands and feet, corns on feet, heels, ruptures and other hurts. Put the snails into a pot, add a good deal of salt and keep it nine days in the ground. After this distil in a glass in the sun.

To make an Ointment for the Cure of the Itch.

Take green corn or broom seed, press the sap therefrom, boil it in the same manner that a mush is cooked, add five cents' worth of sulphur and quarter pound of lard. Rub the body with it every night.

How to make the Genuine Forest Ointment for Healing Gangrene and other Sores.

Take symplocarpus, forest manna, vernonica or speedwell, alsine pubescens, centifolium; press the sap from these herbs, then take white rosin or pitch, tallow and butter; render it down, add the sap and boil together; add five cents' worth of verdigris. This is the genuine forest salve.

To make a Salve when a Man apparently becomes Crooked and causes the Belief that he is Bewitched.

Take parsnip roots and carrots, and make an ointment thereof, and grease the limbs crosswise against the grain of the skin with this mixture.

For a Felon on the Finger.

Take fresh ox gall, boil it, and apply as warm as one can bear it, by dipping the finger therein, and keep it there until it becomes cold. Thus the felon or worm dies soon.

When a Person has a Cancer on Breast or Cheek.

One ounce of sassafras boiled in beer, the pot well sealed, so that the fumes do not evaporate. Drink thereof. If the sore is open, pulverize bones of a corpse, and strew into the wounds. This, also, heals constant discharge from the bladder, etc.

When a Cow's Usefulness is taken, to find out the Person, and mark the same, who caused the Trouble.

On the day of the patron Demetrius, enter a grocery store, buy a steel, purchase and pay for the same without bartering, and have it forged on this very day. The steel must be square, about a span in length, as thick as a foot measure, and, whatever the blacksmith may ask, you must pay. Early in the morning take milk from the cow in the name of God before the witch milks. After this make a fire upon the hearth, put the steel into the fire till it grows red, then take a pair of wooden tongs and draw the steel from the fire, and put the steel into the dish wherein the milk is and keep it there so long till the milk is all evaporated. If the milk is entirely dried out, the witch who caused the mischief must die; but in case the milk is not entirely dried out, the witch will contract blisters upon hands and face, so that she will not be able for a long period to expose herself before the people.

For Hysterics.

Take dried chicken manure, grind it to powder, and give a pinch of it to the patient in a prune. It is a quick remedy.

To Join Stones or Broken Glass.

Take mastich, grind it well with pure water, take the piece of stone or glass, apply the mastich to it, and let it dry, then lift it over a fire to soften the mastich. Put the pieces together and they will become perfectly joined.

Or, take gipsum (plaster of Paris) dissolve in albumen (white of eggs) and smear it on the edges that are to be united. This, too, is a good paste.

To Repair Broken Glasses.

Take half pitch, half rosin, melt together, put on the pieces, put them together, and warm over the fire. It will become solid; then scrape the pitch from the rents and paint them with oil paint.

To make a Water which will Soften all Things.

Take sal ammoniac, nitre and cream of tartar, in equal portions. Let it boil over a quick fire; whatever is put therein will become soft.

To Soften Glass.

Take soluble glass or verre, burn it in a retort to water, and dissolve in this same water some gum arabic; this will so soften the glass, that it may be wrapped up like a cloth.

Or, take eggs, and mix with quick lime, and put the glass therein. It becomes soft in this manner.

An Excellent Hardening.

Take radish wort, as large as you can obtain them, bruise them, and harden in the sap.

Or, take old urine, put the same in a new earthen pot, and let it be boiled down three times to one-half of the original quantity. In this fluid harden most metals.

Also, take acre-worms, called larves, as many as you choose to take, and scurvy-grass in like quantity, boil well together, distil in an alembic just the same as rosewater is distilled. In this substance you can harden whatever you desire.

INDEX TO VOL. I.

A certain Art to kill Flies.................................. 58
Ailments of Cattle, perplexities about.................... 19
Arthritis or Pain in the Limbs............................ 19
Banish Robbers, Murderers and Foes................. 20, 53
Bedbugs, how to drive them away.................... 26, 27
Black Snails, usefulness of................................ 58
Blessing and Grace for all................................. 52
Blood, to still the... 10
Blood, to stop the... 11
Boils or Swellings in the Face......................... 38, 43
Bone, wrenched, dislocated or sprained................ 11
Boots, how to make them waterproof.................. 23
Broken Glass, how to repair........................... 51, 60
Burns, Ointments, for, etc............................. 9, 10
Calves, to wean.. 13
Cancer 17, 22
Cattle, when plagued by Witches......................... 12
Cattle, Pestilence among.................................. 13
Cattle, that no Ill may befall............................ 13
Cattle, Swelling of... 13
Cattle or Horses' Jawbone, when set................... 13
Cattle, Bewitched 13
Cattle, when they cannot make Water.................. 15
Cattle, how to dispose of................................. 52
Cattle, to protect against the Rot...................... 56
Chicken Lice 25
Colic, recipe for..................................... 7, 16, 20, 39, 41
Conflagration, to avoid from Dwelling Houses........ 23
Conflagrations and Epidemics............................ 47
Consumptive Limbs, ointment for........................ 14
Consumptive Lungs 26
Corns, to remove... 13
Costiveness 25
Cough, Remedy to cure a.................................. 38
Cramp, Palsy, and Apparitions............................ 6
Cow, when the Milk leaves the....................... 37, 44
Cow, that she will not bear a Steer, but a Cow Calf.. 13
Cow, Sore Udder and Teats............................... 13
Cow, when she will not change herself.............. 14, 16
Cow, to give a good supply of Milk.................. 14, 15
Cow, to cause her to become Prolific................... 15
Cow, when Blood is in her Milk.......................... 36
Cow, how to restore the usefulness of.................. 54
Cow's usefulness is taken, how to find who caused the trouble 59

INDEX TO VOLUME I.

Cunning Thieves	31
Cut, when a Person is, or Pounded	40
Decay, when the Limb of a Horse becomes less or decays	40
Delivery, when too slow	26
Diarrhœa, when Cattle are Troubled with	54
Dog, to prevent him from becoming Mad	17
Drink for Sick Cattle	57
Dysentery, an easy Remedy for the	16
Engerling Worm or Grub in Sheep	14
Epilepsy or Fits	8, 36, 51
Erysipelas of Animals	12, 26
Erysipelas or St. Anthony's Fire	8
Eye Water, to clear the Sight	25
Eyes, Spots and Cataracts on	57
Fefes, when a Horse has the, Vifes, or Worms	40
Felon on the Finger	59
Fever	18, 39, 43
Fights and Rows	30
Fire Arms, to prevent from being Bewitched	22
Fire, to prevent from going out on the Hearth	42
Fire, to Extinguish without Water	51
Flies, how to kill	58
Forest Ointment, how to make	58
Frosted Feet, to Cure	39
Gall, too much in Cattle	19
Gangrene or Mortification	6, 12
Gangrene of Man and Beast	6
Glass, to Soften	60
Goblins, when plagued by, or ill-disposed People	19
Goitre	42
Golden Ring, by which not only House and Home, but also Man and Beast, are secure against all Misfortunes, Epidemics, and Diseases, and secure against all Wiles of the Devil	29
Gout, and Palsy	36
Gout, Remedy for the	17
Gravel, Remedy for the	15, 18, 41, 45
Griping Pain or Colic	7, 16, 30, 39
Hair to Grow wherever you wish	45
Haish, for the	9
Horses, to Prevent from becoming Stiff	18
Hardening, an Excellent	60
Hard Hearing	25
Haunted Horses or Cattle	19
Headache	22
Hernia or Rupture	42
Horse, to Tame a Balky or Wild	32
How to make Yourself Bold and Amiable	51
Human Being or a Beast, attacked by Evil Spirits	5
Hydrophobia	46
Hysterics, accompanied by Fainting	22, 59

INDEX TO VOLUME I.

Incombustible Oil 27   Impure Air 12
Intestine Colic of Horses................................. 40
Invisible, to make One's Self........................... 27
Itchy Hands, Salve for 45, 58   Jaundice in Cattle 17
Lameness, when Veins are cut or torn.................. 44
Lice and Nits........... 45   Lung Rot of Cattle...... 37
Magnetic Compass, to Discover Buried Treasures.......... 21
Man or Beast attacked by Wicked People................. 5
Man, how to Vanquish.... 52   Mice, how to Destroy... 27
Milk, when a Cow has lost her Milk..................... 14
Milk Thieves 26, 50
Milk of a Cow, when Bloody............................. 36
Milk, when it leaves the Cow........................... 12
Mirror to see what an Enemy designs—distant three or four
    miles 21
Nail, when an Animal treads on......................... 11
Navels of Infants 15   Neuralgia 19
Oil of Earth Worms, how made........................... 58
Ointment for Consumptive Limbs......................... 14
Ointment to open a Boil................................ 38
Ointment for the Cure of the Itch...................... 58
Old Sores on the Feet.................................. 18
Oxen, when a couple of, are to be Trained.............. 32
Pain in the Back....................................... 39
Pains, to Alleviate.................................... 53
Palsy and Epilepsy....... 36   Pestilence 51
Pigeons, how to prevent, from Deserting their Coops....23, 50
Powder for the Gravel.................................. 15
Plaster, for 42, 43
Poison, to draw from a Body............................ 45
Powerful Means, whereby one may Protect Himself against
    Bullet and Sword, against Enemies, or all possible Evil
    and Danger 33
Prevent Persons from doing Evil unto you............... 43
Procreative Organs, to strengthen...................... 39
Protect the Body from the Dangers of Weapons, etc...... 31
Pulmonary Diseases, Consumption, Jaundice, etc......... 57
Punish a Witch that has attacked Cattle................ 55
Putrid Fever, to Save Cattle from...................... 16
Putrid Mouth ....10, 41   Rats and Mice.......... 43
Remedy for Ulcer or Abscess of the Lungs............... 15
Right before a Court of Justice........................ 17
Rupture of a Young Man................................. 8
Rupture of any Animal... 15   Rupture of a Child 36
Saddle which will Press no Horse....................... 25
Salve for Itchy Hands.................................. 45
Salve, when a Man apparently becomes Crooked, how to
    Make 59   Scabs 8

Scars or Pock Marks, to Prevent.................................. 9
Scurvy 25
Secure against Wicked People whilst Traveling............ 41
Secundines of Cow, to Remedy................................... 21
See, how to, in the Darkest Night................................ 27
Shoot securely, upon the Stand, the Chase, or in the Field. 38
Sick Person, to ascertain whether she will Recover...... 45
Sore Breasts 20   Sore Eyes 11
Sore, when it fails to Break Open................................ 14
Sores caused by Pounding or Cutting, when Erysipelas
  follows 39
Speech, when a Man loses, or Tonsils Fall.................. 58
Spiders, House Flies, Gnats, or Mosquitoes, how to banish. 27
Splinter or Thorn Sticking in the Leg......................... 24
Stay a Shot..20, 52
Stitching Pains in Woman or Child............................ 38
Stolen Goods, how to Recover.................................. 37
Stolen Property, to compel a Thief to Return.........20, 54
Stones or Broken Glass, how to Mend....................... 60
Suppuration on Man or Beast.................................... 40
Sweeny in Man or Beast..8, 22
Swelled, when a Person is....................................... 12
Swelled Legs of Horses.. 41
Swelling of Horses ....21, 26   Swelling of the Body.... 14
Swellings 10, 19, 38
That Nobody may Hurt you—how to be Secure against
  Assailants 33   Thief, to Detect........ 17
Thief, to Fasten a........ 24   Toothache 24, 42, 52
Treasures, to Discover Buried.................................. 22
Treasures, how they beneath the Earth Rise and Fall... 21
Udder of a Cow, when Bewitched.............................. 16
Urine, to tell by the, all Diseases.............................. 48
Vine Fretters and Wall Lice, to drive away................. 40
Virility of Manhood, how to Restore.......................... 46
Warts or Tumors.. 43
Water, when Unable to Pass................................20, 26
Water, for one who cannot Hold his........................ 14
Water, to make a, which will Soften all Things........ 60
Weather, how to Prognosticate................................ 50
White Swelling and Joint Water (Hydrospy)............ 40
Wild Fire of Man and Beast..................................... 9
Wine, how to Clarify. Wines, how to Improve In-
  ferior 28, 29, 47
Witches, to know when Cattle are Plagued by.......... 12
Worm in any part of the Body................7, 21, 26, 52
Wounds and Stopping of Blood................................ 11
Wounds, Fresh 20
Wounded, to Prevent from being............................. 45

ALBERTUS MAGNUS

BEING THE APPROVED, VERIFIED, SYMPATHETIC AND NATURAL

EGYPTIAN SECRETS

OR,

WHITE AND BLACK ART FOR MAN AND BEAST

THE BOOK OF NATURE AND THE HIDDEN SECRETS
AND MYSTERIES OF LIFE UNVEILED; BEING THE

Forbidden Knowledge of Ancient Philosophers

By that celebrated Student, Philosopher, Chemist, Naturalist, Psychomist, Astrologer, Alchemist, Metallurgist, Sorcerer, Explanator of the Mysteries of Wizards and Witchcraft; together with recondite Views of numerous Arts and Sciences—Obscure, Plain, Practical, Etc., Etc.

TRANSLATED FROM THE GERMAN

CONTENTS OF VOL. II.

Chiefly many Horse Cures—To Restore the Sight to Blind Horses—to Cure Broken Legs of Horses—To Cite Witches—More than Ten different Methods to Mark Witches—How to Prevent Witches from Entering a Stable—To Cure Man or Beast of the Bites of Rabid Animals—Ointments for Burns—For Toothache—For the Gout—For Asthma—For Neuralgia—For Consumption—To Heal Ruptures—To Cure Epilepsy—To Heal Unhealthy Discharges, and many other Cures.

EGYPTIAN PUBLISHING CO.

CHICAGO.

TO THE READER

The recipes noted in this book have been successfully applied, used and approved of, by an experienced man for many years, and have been found to be very appropriate remedies; and hence they may be recommended to every one who will use them with care, provided such person has the true belief. These important remedies would have still remained unpublished, had it not been for the fact that the proprietor of the same had the inclination to assist an unfortunate family with the result of this publication, and thus it happened that they were printed, and that perishing family derive the benefit from the sale of this book by obtaining a livelihood, and the public are also benefited thereby. Inasmuch as, at this juncture, all looks so gloomy in society, the writer of this expects that no pirate of books will wrongfully seize this work and reprint the same, if such an one does not wish to incur the eternal curse, and even condemnation from such an act. While we recommend it to the protection of God and the Holy Trinity, that they may be watching the same, and set the Angel Michael as watch and guard over the undertaking, so that no pirate may rob the real and legal owner of the means of deriving his daily bread from the sale of this publication, and cheat him of his property by the peril of losing his blessedness; such a being would never find rest nor quiet, by day or night, neither here below nor in the hereafter, by seeking to defraud the publisher of his own. This would God the Father, Son, and Holy Spirit grant.

Mirathe saepy Satonich petanish pistau ytmye higarin ygeirion temgaron—aycon, dunsnas caflilacias satas claeius jocony, hasihaja yeynino Stephatitas beaae Ind, Doneny eya hidue reu vialta eye vahaspa Saya Salna bebia euci yaya Elencke na vena Serna.

(Signed)

Albertus Magnus.

ALBERTUS MAGNUS

OR

EGYPTIAN SECRETS

For the Swelling of the Cattle.

Whatever I embrace with my right arm, that it may not receive any harm; and three times move with the right hand over the back; † † † To be recited three times. Probatum.

For the Fever.

Take the water of the patient and mix it with some flour and make a dough thereof, of which seventy-seven small cakes are made, each one as large as a lintel; proceed before sunrise to an ant-hill and throw the cakes therein. As soon as the insects have devoured the cakes, the fever vanishes. Probatum.

For Cataract of the Eye.

Take half an ounce of prepared tutia, and blow this through a goose quill into the animal's eyes.

For Spots in the Eye.

Take two drachms tutia, half drachm white vitriol, one half of an ounce rose honey, make a salve thereof, and use it to grease the eyes therewith.

To Heal Boils on the Hoofs.

Take two ounces of nitric spirit, one drachm of sperm oil, mix well, and steep the boil in it. After this rub with the Egyptian salve.

To make a good Ointment for Burns.

Take two ounces of turpentine, three ounces of yellow bees'-wax, six ounces of linseed oil; mix upon a coal fire and grease the sore therewith.

For Falling of the Womb and Cough.

Take orange peels, aloes one drachm, and five cents' worth of carrots. Put in a bottle, shake well, and take evenings and mornings a good draught of it till the cure is effected.

To stop the Bleeding of a Wound.

Paint the wound with nitric spirit.

To make a Blister.

Take cantharides (Spanish fly powder), 4 ounces; turpentine, 8 ounces; yellow bees'-wax, 4 ounces; linseed oil, 6 ounces. Mix these ingredients to a plaster.

To Extirpate Warts.

Take blossoms of the walnut tree, rub the warts with them, and they will soon heal.

To cite a Witch.

Take an earthen pot, not glazed, yarn spun by a girl not yet seven years old. Put the water of the bewitched animal into the pot, then take the egg of a black hen and some of the yarn and move the latter three times round the egg, and ejaculate in the three devils' name; after this put the egg into the water of the pot, seal the lid of the vessel tightly that no fumes may ooze therefrom, but observe that the head of the lid is below. While setting the pot upon the fire, pronounce the following: Lucifer, devil summon the sorcerer before the witch or me, in the three devils' name.

In Case one Suffers from a Theft.

If something is stolen from you, proceed also as stated above, take likewise water, draw it from a brook stream downward, and cut three splinters from the threshold over which the thief did run. The water must be drawn in the three names of the devil.

That no Witch may leave a Church.

Purchase a pair of new shoes, grease them on Saturday with grease on the outer sole, then put them on and walk to the church, and no witch can find the way out of the church without you proceed before her.

Of Witches and Sorcery.

Fasten a squill (sea onion) over the principal door of the house, and no person will come to trouble you in the dwelling.

To Beat Witches.

Let the sweepings, which are swept together in a house for three days remain in a heap, and on the third day cover it with a black cloth made of drilling, then take a stick of an elm tree and flog the dirt heap bravely, and the sorceress must assist, or you will batter her to death. Probatum.

For Sorcery.

Take elmwood on a Good-Friday, cut the same while calling the holiest names. Cut chips of this wood from one to two inches in length. Cut upon them, in the three holiest names, three crosses. † † † Wherever such a slip is placed, all sorcery will be banished.

To Cause a Witch to Die within One Minute.

First, try to obtain a piece of the heart of the cattle which had been attacked, then take a little butter and fry the piece therein, as if prepared for eating, then take three nails from the coffin of a corpse, and pierce with them the heart through and through. Piercing the heart and killing the witch, are facts of the same moment. All will be correct at once. Good and approved.

To Burn a Witch so that she receives Pock Marks over her entire Body.

Take butter from the household larder, render it down in an iron pan until it broils, then take ivy or wintergreen, and fry it; take three nails of a coffin and stick them in that sauce; carry the mass to a place where neither sun nor moon shines into, and the witch will be sick for half of a year.

When a Horse is Sick or has the Blind Fistula.

Take of camphor, for five cents; saffron, five cents; olive oil, five cents, and give it in a glass of wine. It helps certain sure.

For Influenza, Toothache, and Headache.

I implore thee, by the living God, that thou may draw the disease from the body of N. N., and hurt him as little as it did hurt the Lord Jesus to be crucified; this commands you God the Father, Son and Holy Spirit. Three times spoken.

A Magic for One who has been Infatuated by Illicit Love to a Female.

Such a person must put a pair of shoes on, and walk therein until his feet perspire, but must walk fast, so that the feet do not smell badly; then take off the right shoe, drink some beer or wine out of this shoe, and he will from that moment lose all affection for her.

A Banishment.

Three trees are standing on Jesus' heart—the first is called humility, the other forbearing, the third is called, if it pleases, God. Rider, horse, or walker on foot, ye shalt not stand still, and not move from hence until I grant permission.

While pronouncing this, the hat must be placed on the back of the head, and the right hand put three times thereto. When designing to release them, grasp the hat with the left hand, and put the hat as it was before, keep the hat in the left hand and beat with the hat in the direction where they are wanted to move to or remove from hence.

The sufferings of Christ I bear upon me. Oh! trouble leave me, I hold thee fast for Christ's sake and blood, that removes all ill from me, by his sweat and death, by his holy five wounds so red, through his resurrection and ascension to heaven may give that God will protect me as long as I live. † † †

To Stay a Rider or Several Horsemen.

In meekness I begin my work, stop rider, walker, robber stop, stop ye thieves. In meekness desist, from evil shrink, since Jesus' blood did we drink; your musket and your rifle be stopped with Jesus' blood, your sabres, knives, swords, helbards and spear, they be as soft as Christ's five holy wounds. Since only three roses upon the Saviour's heart do bloom, the first is benign, the second of good mind, the third is the will of God. While ye remain under these flowers, ye must stand still as long as I will, but not through me, but for the sake of God the Father, God the Son, and God the Holy Spirit, ye are conjured and banished. † † †

While pronouncing grace reverse the knife in your trouser pocket, and tie a knot in your shirt or your handkerchief.

If you wish to let them ride away again, speak. Ride thither in the bad name of all evil spirits.

To Cause the Return of Stolen Property.

Take three pieces of bread, three pinches of salt and three pieces of hog's lard, make a strong flame, put all the articles upon this fire, and say the following words, while keeping alone:

I put bread, salt and lard for the thief upon the fire, for thy sin and temerity so dire. I place them upon thy lungs, liver and heart, that thou art troubled with terror and smart, a distress shall come over thee with dread as if thou wert to be smitten dead, all veins in thy body shall burst and break, and great havoc and trouble shall make, that thou shalt have no peace nor rest, till what thou hast stolen thou hast returned and brought all back from whence it were taken. Three times to recite and every time the three holiest names spoken.

For the Toothache.

Bay leaf flour for five cents; fennel powder for five cents. A handful wheaten flour and one egg; bake a cake of this, and put upon the ears during the night.

To Lay Spirits by an Anathema.

Ye persons look upon me for a moment till I draw three blood drops from you, which ye have forfeited. The first I draw from your teeth, the other from your lung, the third I draw from your heart's own main; with this I take your hosts away and ye shall stand till I remove from ye the iron band. † † † Three times spoken.

Another Anathema.

Welcome, ye brethren, be of good cheer, we have partaken of Christ's blood there and here, and if we had not drank it, yet we surely would do so when next time we met. God the Father who is with me, God the Son who is with thee, God the Holy Spirit who is between us all, that we in peace may part, in peace may call, that never a sword ye may be able to draw, no pistol may fire, no rifle nor cannon discharge. God aid me to vanquish you all.

For the Mange or Itch of Sheep.

Black tobacco, fir-wood; linden-wood, pigeon manure; chicken fat, aquafortis, oil of turpentine; rapeseed oil, aquafortis, aloes; equal parts of each. Make an ointment of these articles and grease the sheep therewith.

For the Purging of the Sheep.

Laurel oil and excecizium made into a salve, and the body greased with it; Spanish fly, five cents; laurel oil, five cents; evorbium, five cents; lard one quart, and three-points of a knife full of salt. All of these mix cold and grease several days in succession.

For a Rupture.

Take red bolus and cognac brandy, make a plaster thereof, smear upon some sheepskin, and apply the same to the affected spot while warm.

For the Chicken Pox.

A certain cure for this disease, to save the eyes of the children, take roots of rue and roots of sassafras, and suspend them from the child's neck. Probatum est.

To Prevent every Person from Hitting the Target.

Put a splinter of wood which has been hit by a thunder bolt behind the target. No person will be able to hit such a target.

To cause Rifles or Muskets to miss Fire.

Speak these words: AFA AFCA NOSTRA, when you are able to look into the barrel of some person's gun and it will fail to discharge; but if you desire it to give fire recall these words backward.

EGYPTIAN SECRETS.

To prevent a Person from Firing a Gun while you are looking into the Barrel.

Pronounce: PAX SAX SARAX.

To make One's Self Shot Proof.

Dig and stick mouse-ear herb on a Friday, during the half or full of the moon, tie in a white cloth and suspend it from the body. Probatum.

Or carry these words upon your body: LIGHT, BETTER, CLOTENTAL, SOBATH, ADONAY, ALBOA, FLORAT.

To Compel a Dog, Horse, or other Animal to Follow You.

Casper guide thee, Balthasar bind thee, Melchior keep thee, three times. These words utter into the right ear.

To compel a Thief to Return Stolen Articles.

Upon this stone I pray to the Lord, that he may give me three nails upon my word, the first I hammer through his tongue, the other through his heart and his lung, the third through all his limbs and his members, that the thief to return the things may remember, that he may have neither peace nor rest like the Virgin Mary bore her child upon straw, in the name of God the Father, the Son, and the Holy Spirit.

To prevent a Person to Escape.

Take a needle wherewith the gown of a corpse was sewed, and draw this needle through the hat or shoe of him whom you seek to fasten, and he cannot escape.

For a Horse that cannot Stall.

Take hare leap herb, tie a stone to it, and let the horse drink over it, and forthwith the horse will have an opening.

To See what Others cannot See.

Take a cat's eye, lay it in salt water, let it remain there for three days, and then for six days into the rays of the sun, after this have it set in silver, and hang it around your neck.

To Draw Moles from their Holes.

Take sulphur and garlic, place it over the holes, and the moles must come out immediately.

To Obtain Money.

Take the eggs of a swallow, boil them, return them to the nest, and if the old swallow brings a root to the nest, take it, put it into your purse, and carry it in your pocket, and be happy.

To Open Locks.

Kill a green frog, expose it to the sun for three days, powder or pulverize it. A little of this powder put into a lock will open the same.

To Understand the Song of Birds.

Take the tongue of a vulture, lay it for three days and three nights in honey, afterward under your tongue, and thus you will understand all the songs of birds.

To Stop the Bleeding of a Wound.

Take a small bone of a human body and put into the wound, and the blood will cease to flow.

To Drive away Bed Bugs.

Take the scrapings of the hoof which the farrier cuts when shoeing a horse, boil them well in water, with it wash the bedsteads or whatever may be infested with the pests. Has been satisfactorily tried.

To Purchase Cheaply and Sell at a High Price.

Catch a white weasel, take its head off, and carry in your right side pocket. Probatum.

When a Horse has a Skin growing over the Retina of the Eye.

Take of fresh butter a piece as large as a pigeon's egg and knead with saffron. Put it into the eye of the horse, bandage the eye, and in twenty-four hours the skin will have vanished.

Take one pound of fresh butter, which has not been watered, put it into a pan, heat it, bake twenty cakes of it, keep the lard for future use. A spoonful of the same put into a beverage for a drink, and to desist from drinking anything else, and used as long as is desired, will cure. Probatum.

To Sharpen Scythes for Mowing.

R. kitr., arvitr., romain erad, vitr., alb., [] r erad, of each for five cents, all pulverized, and some of it always kept nights in a dish put upon the grindstone, and sharpen therewith the scythe, and it will be in good condition for mowing.

For Bites of Rabid Dogs.

Write these words upon a letter, and hang the same around the neck of man or beast:

† Paga † Chaga † Pagula † Chagula † Pagula; has been tried on man or beast.

How to Discern all Secrets and Invisible Things.

If you find a white adder under a hazelnut shrub, which had twelve other vipers as its twelve guardsmen with it, and the hazelnut bush, under which they lay, bears commonly medlers, you must eat the white adder with your other food, and you will be enabled to see and discern all secret and otherwise hidden things.

How a Midwife in Nuremberg Stopped the Blood of Patients.

Jesus born at Bethlehem, Jesus crucified at Jerusalem, as true as these words are, to truly understand N. N. (here call the name of him whom you desire to help) that thy blood will now be stopped, in the name of God the Father, the Son, and the Holy Spirit.

To make yourself Shot Proof.

Dig and stitch mouse-ear roots on a Friday, during full moon or half moon, tie it in a white handkerchief, and wear it around the neck. Probatum.

Or this: Carry the following words on your person: Light, Beff, Cletemati, Adonai, Cleona, Florit.

Another.

In June, on SS. Peter and Paul's Day, dig blue waywort roots, fifteen minutes before twelve o'clock; also procure the herb of this plant. If you carry this herb with you, and they bind or fetter you, all ropes, fetters and locks, will spring open; neither can you be shot.

Or: Take wild radishes, eat them before breakfast, and no one will be able to flog you, and while you carry them in your mouth you will be able to vanquish all your enemies.

Or: He who can devour his own salicin, he is entirely unconquerable.

How to make One's Self Agreeable to All.

Carry a whoop's eye on your person. If you carry it in front of your breast, all your enemies will become kind to you, and if you carry it in your purse you make a good bargain on all what you sell.

To Fasten a Person that he may not Escape.

Take a needle wherewith the gown from a corpse had been sewed and put this needle into the foot prints of the person you seek to fasten. And never will that person, so treated, be able to get away.

To have Good Luck in Playing, and how to make Yourself Liked by People.

Take the right thumb in your hand, and put the hand in your right-hand pocket whenever a delinquent is executed, and thus you will secure good luck in playing and be liked by your fellow-men.

To Prevent Hares from Destroying the Cabbage.

Take garlic, press out the sap, sprinkle over cabbage seed and sow the same. Probatum.

To Try if a Person is Chaste.

Sap of radish squeezed into the hand will prove what you wish to know. If they do not fumble or grabble they are all right.

How to Cause your Intended Wife to Love you.

Take feathers from a rooster's tail, press them three times into her hand. Probatum.

Or: Take a turtle dove tongue into your mouth, talk to your friend agreeably, kiss her and she will love you so dearly that she cannot love another.

When you wish that your Sweetheart shall not deny you.

Take the turtle dove tongue into your mouth again and kiss her, and she will accept your suit.

Or: Take salt, cheese and flour, mix it together, put it into her room, and she will have no rest until she sees you.

An Ambrose-stone.

Steal the eggs of a raven, boil them hard, lay them again into the nest and the raven will fly across the sea and bring a stone from abroad and lay it over the eggs and they will become at once soft again. If such a stone is wrapped up into a bay leaf and is given to a prisoner, that prisoner will be liberated at once. Whoever touches a door with such a stone, to him that door will be opened, and he who puts that stone into his mouth will understand the song of every bird.

To Stop the Blood of One whose Name is only Known.

Three roses are under our beloved Master's heart; the first is humility, the second gentleness. Oh, blood with N. N., stand still, is what our Lord asks, and his will. † † †

When a Horse is Costive.

Give it horseradish, enzian and Christmas roots.

For Burns.

I have been burnt, Christ the Lord was crucified. If to him the crucifying did no harm, the burning will not harm thee. † † † But if you do it for some other person speak thus: Thou hast burnt thyself, N. N. If you are not near this person you may nevertheless aid him if you only know his name.

Take unwatered butter and move it round the burnt spot, and after this put the butter for nine days in a quiet, secluded place.

An Approved Representation.

Bind Peter, bind Peter, bind Peter, bind for me all those thieves, both male and female, who steal from my home or my estates, or have the intention of doing so, bind them with iron bands and with the Lord's own hands, with the holy five wounds, and with the true twelve hours, that they must stand for me like a stick and look like a buck, count for me the stars that stand in the firmament, they look upon the Lord's foliage, herbage and grass, which groweth on earth, the heaven be their cover, the earth be their shoe. If ye are stronger than God then ye may from hence depart, but in case ye are not stronger than God, stand still until I free you by my will. For this may give aid God the Father, God the Son and God the Holy Spirit.

Solution.

Go ye in the name of our Lord Jesus Christ, whence you come from, to this end help ye God the Father, God the Son and God the Holy Spirit.

When Something is Stolen from You, how to Cause its Return.

Take a bit of bread and a pinch of salt also a piece of lard, and put all these things upon the fire and flame, and speak: This all I put into the fiery glow, for all thy sin and haughtiness; the lard shall cause thy veins to break, the salt shall embitter thy life, that your tongue will smart and blister, and smarting, galling be to you that bread as if thou shouldst be stricken dead. In the name of God the Father, God the Son and God the Holy Spirit. Three times spoken and before three times twenty-four hours will elapse, he (the thief) will be there, and you tell him to depart in the name of God.

For Bed Bugs in Bedsteads.

One ounce mercury, two ounces hog's lard rendered down, then take a drachm of bruised wolfswort, one drachm juniperberry oil, make into a salve and apply the same to the cracks and screw-holes of the bedsteads. A good remedy. Probatum.

An Excellent way to Prove whether a Person is a Witch or not.

First. Try to obtain St. John's roots and one ounce of herb of the same plant called moto. Write the following letters upon a scrap of paper and put to the root and herbs:

S A T O R † Cross of Christ mildepos
A R E P O † Cross of Christ mesepos
T E N E T † Cross of Christ Habenepos
O P E R A
R O T A S

This must be sewed up in a piece of leather, and if you wish to see the witch, only carry the paper with you, but it must be taken in the hour when the first quarter of the moon occurs.

You will then perceive that no witch can remain in the same room with you.

If a Horse has Eaten too much and is Swelled.

Take from four to five pounds of fresh milk; mix a few pinches of black snuff tobacco in the milk, or instead of the tobacco some vinegar and ground leaven or yeast. This give to the sick animal, whereupon it should be slowly driven around. The horse will soon have an opening, and is saved in an easy manner from the disease.

When an Animal is Sprained on the Shoulder Blade or in any other Limb or Member.

In order to dispose of the curdled blood it is necessary to mix an equal part of mutton tallow with turpentine. Grease the limb therewith and rub gently.

When a Child is Bewitched.

Stand with the child toward the morning sun, and speak: Be welcome in God's name and sunshine, from whence didst brightly beam, aid me and my dear child and feign my songs serenely stream. To God the Father sound my praise, help praise the Holy Ghost that he restore my child to health, I praise the heavenly host. † † †

For the Erysipelas.

Take a quart of fresh milk, dog's waste stirred therein and strained through a cloth. This is a good internal medicine.

Or make for External Use:

Tormantil wort	1 drachm
Dragon blood	2 ounces
Red chalk stone	1 drachm

Mix together and put in milk.

For Sore Feet.

Wounds so good, I stop your smart with God's own blood, that ye never swell, nor fester, till the dear mother of God shall bear another son. † † † Satora robote Netabe ratotta. S. † † †

To Compel a Thief to Return Stolen Property.

In the name of the Holy Trinity, I urge and conjure, N. N., thou thief, male or female thief, in the name of God who knows all, through Aaron the high priest, through whose aid I compel and vanquish all devils, this be imparted to you, Moloch and, Lucifer too will be sent, as also St. Michael, St. Gabriel, St. Raphael with many thousand legions of obedient spirts and holy angels of God, this be thy compulsion, thy obedience, this be thy ransom, this be thy plague, this be thy obligation: Asteroth, God in Gods and of God, the thief who robbed N. N., that thief, be it male or female, bring hither to me in my N. N. house with the articles stolen. Beelzubub be bound, Lucifer be bound. Satan be bound with the rays which emanate from the holy countenance of God; the God who hath given to Moses the commandments, he would aid me, N. N., out of trouble, he dishonor you! But I who keep the commandment, love the law, that law be God, a powerful God, a conqueror, a comforter and savior. Moloch, Lucifer, Asteroth Pemeoth Forni gator, Anector, Somiator, sleep ye not, awake, the strong hero Holaha, the powerful Eaton, the mighty Tetragramaton; Athe, Alpha et Omega, compel ye that the thief may return the stolen articles into the house of N. N., and that the thief shall have neither rest nor peace through sand and land, through sea or air, on mountain or rock, thou accursed devil, lead the thief back into my house with all the stolen goods.

Behold the mighty God, St. Zapheel be thy prayer, be thy compulsion, the ark of God, the ark of the covenant of the dwelling of the Lord shall aid me to bring the rope for ye devils, and for this be God in God my helper in need and trouble. Jehovah, Saboah, Emanuel, ah Jathos Noio sottis, Ishiros, Kiriel aios Fius Imago Via veritas Salvator Oberator Tetragramatum Stoch Nahus tribelasus Spenter omnipotens Venus, Sanitus, Trinus, Imenesus, Virtus, Principitatis, Liberator Manus Erohye, Mediator Imbrator Oulus Prillus, teris Judaea arnes humuisien. Psalm 91. Pray; Satan, thou accursed devil, hast thou heard the power of Adonay, our great Lord, then thou must through the power of Jehovah at once compel the thief who has robbed N. N. and force him (or her) that these stolen things be returned into my N.•N.'s house.

Immanuel is thy commander, Sada drive thee with the thief into my house. Ishiros force thee, agios Imperator Dominus

God Alpha and Omega may send his heavenly power, Cherubim and Seraphim, these mighty princes of heaven. St. Michael, St. Gabriel, St. Sephael, St. Uriel the transparent and penetrating mediator be mediator between thee and me. Hereby I conjure the thief that thou be obedient and tractable like the lightning's flash, obedient to Almighty God; to this end help me, God Father, Son and Holy Spirit.

When a Cow has Calved or has the Fever and to Prevent that her Milk be taken During that Year.

After the cow has calved, the appended words should be given, and when the animal has the fever a letter must be suspended on her a Friday between the hours of twelve and one. The letters taken three days in succession at an uneven hour is probatum.

```
S A T O R
A R E P O
T E N E T
O P E R A
R O T A S
```

To Allay Pains Wherever they be.

To-day is a holy sacred day, that God will not cause you any pain to bear, which thou may have on any part of your body, be it man, horse, cattle, or anything living, all the same.

† God greet thee dear son † Edward.
† God greet thee dear spouse Otto.
† God greet thee son, Holy Spirit
Tetragramatum.

I beseech thee. Oh, holy Trinity, help this N. N., that all his pains may cease, whatever they may be called and all that cometh from evil things. Christ commandeth, Christ vanquisheth, Christ became a being in flesh for thy sake and to protect thee against all evil. Jesus Christ of Nazareth, the crucified Saviour, with Mary his beloved mother, help this N. N. from all evil whatever name it may bear. Amen. † † † Jesus Nazarenus Rex Judaeorum.

For a Costive Cow.

Take cleanswort, sage, meadow mint, hedge turnips, bruise and mix them well and boil in three quarts of water; also put a rusty rick into the water as well as three hands full of salt while pronouncing the three holiest names.

After this do for the Colic as follow

Body, I conjure thee, by the holy gospel and the holy three, that thou wilt move into the rightful place and bed; or thou wilt cause both me N. N. and my cow a certain death. † † † This three times repeated is surely Probatum.

For a Fractured Leg and Open Sores.

Whoever fractures a leg or receives any other injury from a fall, etc., should say the following prayer and grace three times over the injured part, as will be taught hereafter, by N. N., pronounce the man's name and bend the leg toward the rising sun: N. N., I will bend and smooth thy leg and keep it free from all wild flesh and maggots fresh, this shall allay all terrible sores and smarts. At the entrance to my right I behold a sinner on the cross, whose legs and arms were bent and broken, in the middle I behold our Saviour meek, whom the nails did not in the least cause pain; as true as in the holy cross taken no limb nor bone nor his leg was broken. I now in the name of the mediator I will cure all sores and breaks will heal, that they be well as heretofore, may they be caused by falling shooting or magic, sores by arms of lead, glass, silver, steel or ore. It shall be done as surely as St. John has baptized the holy man.

OFANO, OBLAMO, OSPERGO.

These three names should be always pronounced after the above grace, instead of the three holy names.

How to Cure a Fractured Leg.

When a human being or any animal fractures an arm or leg, set it first that it may meet correctly together; after this is done lay both of your hands around the fracture and pronounce the following grace three times over the same and shingle the limb and bandage it, that it may stay well together and not draw apart, the leg will heal with God's help, as it had been heretofore.

Speak also thus:

Broken leg may God the Father heal thee, be healed in the name of God the Son, it heal thee, the Holy Spirit. Grant God that thou shouldst be like stone or bone, as thou hast been before. This help the dear Lord Jesus Christ, whom never a bone did break. † † † Three times. Probatum.

To cut a Stick wherewith to drive away Moles and to flog a Person.

When new moon comes on a Tuesday, go early in the morning, before the sun rises, to a hazelnut shrub which grew in one year, bend thy face toward the sun and cut this stick in three cuts, in the three highest names, and speak the appended words. When you come to a mole's hill, put your jacket upon that mole's hill, and flog the same bravely and no mole will throw up earth, and you will also give a flogging to a person by calling his name, in the same manner.

HOLA NOA MASSA.

When an Animal is Stupid.

When an animal is stupid, when it runs around as if it had the rams, or when it carries the head upon one side, which signifies a sort of woe or pain, it may arise from heat and superfluous blood; hence it would be good to bleed such a beast three or four times, especially on a Friday. In all cases, however an animal should suffer from such an ailment, pronounce the following grace three times over it, the first time stand upon the right side of the animal; the second time its left side; the third time again upon the right side, and while saying the grace move constantly your hand over the back of the animal.

Blood forget thy motion, just as our Lord God does unto a man who on the Sabbath day stands still and not listen to the holy gospel's will. † † †

For Worms and Colic.

Heart worm, fruit worm and colic, I command you by the holy judgment of the Lord, that ye shall quietly lay and **never** move, nor stay, till the mother of God is heard from again.

For Lung Disease.

When the lung disease rages in any place, a good remedy and preventive for healthy cattle is the following: Write the words given below upon a piece of paper and make thereof a cylindric bag and put therein the powder hereunto described, and let the cattle take it evenings after feeding them, but only once, and such cattle will not catch the contagion. But in case the cattle is already sick, give three evenings in succession such a package and it will become well again.

N. N., here pronounce the name of the cattle, thus I write and prescribe for thy lungs, as also for the rot, in the name of the Father, the Son and Holy Spirit.

This latter is to be written upon paper and the mentioned roll made thereof, therein put lung herbs as grows on the trunks of oak trees, juniper berries and the upper branches of juniper shrubs, as one as much as of the other, dry it and then pulverize, and of this powder take three good pinches. put the same in the three highest names in the cylinder roll and give it to the cattle evenings after feeding time with the paper as has been described above. This and confidence in God will surely help.

For the Colic.

Colic, I embrace thee, colic, I surround thee, I denounce that from this flesh and blood now flee. Beware thee, God, blood and flesh the heavenly host; save thee God the Holy Ghost.

For Flush and Neuralgic Pains of Man and Beast.

Flush and rush, I conjure thee, three fathoms beneath the earth to flee, thus pray N. N., to the Lord, that the ailment vanish and banish henceforth, until the mother of God another son will bear and thus thy pain shall vanish I swear. † † †

For the Stirring.

Buy a cord for one cent, quiet homeward thy footsteps bent. then some knots drawn on that cord, with it hit without speaking one word the side of the bail but never the top without fail.

For Influenza in the Eyes of Man or Beast.

I too beseech thee in the name of God, the Father, Son and Holy Spirit. Influenza I mean thee, that thou may vanish and cease and my body release, as the body in the grave, cease by night and by day, like the body in the grave does decay. † † †

Pray the Lord's prayer, one creed, and aid me helper, bless in pangs and distress.

A sure Remedy for Children having Measles so that they may not Lose their Eyesight.

Roots of rue, roots of sabisses, hang around the neck of the patient, is probatum.

When a Cow is Costive.

Boil linseed in water, give it as a drink to the cow. It will surely help.

For the Palsy.

God greet thee, thou cold, cold face, in the name of God and the judgment day, through God and the Holy Spirit shalt thou depart from this flesh and blood, in the name of God the Father, and the Son and the Holy Spirit; three Fridays in succession; on every occasion, three times to repeat.

A Verse for the Hair Worm.

God the Lord went Zacre, upon a fertile acre, he made three furrows, he caught three worms. The first is the battle worm, the other the gnat worm, the third is the hair worm; battle worm, gnat worm, and hair worm rush from out this flesh worm. † † †

An Approved Oil for Lame Limbs.

Take wool, herb flowers, put them into a glass, and after this in an ant hill one knee deep, and tie a bladder around the glass. Let the glass remain there for ten days and the contents will turn to water, wherewith anoint the limbs whenever they pain.

For the Gravel, a simple but efficient Art.

Boil a broth of Eben herbs; drink of this, morning and evening. Eben herbs is transecantia virginica. This cure is excellent.

To Cure Warts.

Rub the wart with nut blossoms till they heal.

To make an Herb Wine.

1. Horse Radish.
2. Rockmoss Flowers.
3. Stone Flowrets.
4. Coxcomb.
5. Veronica.
6. Rue.
7. Sage.
8. Grape Hyacinth.
9. Lung Wort;

of each a handful; five cents' worth of rose blood, one-half pound of barley, one quart of water and one quart of wine, wherein the herbs have to be boiled until one pint evaporates. Drink morning and evening one glassful thereof.

When a Woman Suffers from not being Regular.

Boil the wood of red grapes in red or white wine, and let the person drink it.

To drive Boils and Swellings away.

Go to a butcher, who is about slaughtering a cow, speak to him, but beseech him three times for the sake of God, give me the bladder containing the water. Let the water after this run out, so that the water of the sick man may run into the bladder; thereupon hang the bladder in the smoke with the water in it. It will surely help.

For the Gout or Sweeny of Man and Beast.

If you have gout in your body, between skin and flesh, then help you God the Father, Son and Holy Spirit. As little as God the Father was gouty as little shalt thou be gouty, neither the Holy Trinity had the gout, this be, for the seventy-seven times gout, a good cure. † † †

When a Cow Loses her Milk.

Go to the potter and buy a new pot, do not ask the price, but give him twenty-five cents or more; thereupon catch the cow's water in the pot, and pour it into a good trough, stop the key-hole up. Take a tile, paste it in front and rear, then take a few glasses of milk from the cow and pour into the tile, make a fire under it, and when the milk boils, take the water pour it into the milk; take a new broom which had never been used, with it hit bravely therein, and if you wish to hit the witch still better, then take the broom-handle and flog bravely upon the vessel.

Excellent Drops for the Stomach.

Take ten cents' worth of castoreum, five cents worth of cinnamon, five cents' worth of cloves, twenty cents' worth of chinin, three cents' worth of nutmeg, five cents' worth of enzian root, and a little orange peel. Distil in a pint of alcohol. Let it draw in a temperate warmth for a few weeks, then filter through paper, and let it run into a glass bottle. The species fill up with fresh alcohol, and let it stand until again ready for use, then filter and so forth.

To Prevent Anybody from taking Anything belonging to you.

Inscribe the appended letters upon a stick, and put it thereto:

† Z. † D. I. A. † B. † Z. † S. A.
B. Z. † H. V. W. F. † B. E. R. S. † † †

For Frosted Feet.

Take deer's tallow, one ounce of virgin wax, and one ounce laurel oil. Let these run together, add a little brandy, smear upon three plasters, and apply to the feet. It is a sure cure.

When a Horse stubbornly refuses to be Shod, speak into his Ear.

† Caspar raise thee. Melchior bind thee. † Balthasar surround thee. † † †

This formula may also be used when a piece of cattle strays away or for making game stand. It will only be necessary to say, by the last name, where it may be wanted: Balthasar conduct thee back.

For the Worm on the Finger.

Write the following words upon a paper, and tie it around the sore finger, or the horse's hindquarters, wherever the worm is, and it will die: Afriass, aesteias, Srus, Srus, Sras, Atestoos, Xaaja † se do † da da † Abia Am bles † Greem Er A. ran † C y y † Um † † †

For the Salt Rheum.

Camphor, five cents; olive oil, five cents; white lead, five cents some silver litherage, and a little wine vinegar. Make into a salve paint on a plaster, and apply.

To Transfix a Rider.

In the name of the Holy Trinity, God Father, God Son, God the Holy Spirit, here I fasten thee, rider and warrior. Mother Mary shall decide over you. The paradise is opened unto him. Therewith I am closed with my goods and chattels. Hold therein hellish fire flames, as true as Christ was crucified upon the cross.

Solution.

With these words, by which I fixed you, I again release thee. † † †

Another formula for the Same.

Horse and rider, I affix ye, and by the holy three hours. Horse and rider, I fix ye, by the holy five words and wounds, as Jesus Christ spake while on the Cross. God the Father will cause thee to appear, God the Son will bind thee, and God the Holy Ghost will not liberate thee until I bid thee to depart hence. † † †

To Fix a Thief.

Mary walked with her dear child, when two thieves came by, and quickly took it away from her. But Mary spake to St. Peter: St. Peter, St. Peter bind. St. Peter said: I have bound him with Jesus' bands, with his five holy wounds my goods have bound. Whoever steals from me, shall stand like a stick, and look around like a buck. If he can count more than all the stars which stand on the sky, can count all leaves, all blades of grass, all drops of rain, all flakes of snow, he may depart with his stolen goods. If he cannot do this, he stands on this place for a ransom, until I may be able to view him with my own eyes, and with my own mouth bid him to go thither.

Solution.

Depart in the name of the Holy Trinity.

To Make a Mirror in which Everything may be Discerned.

Procure a looking glass, such as are commonly sold. Inscribe the characters noted below upon it. Inter it on the crossing of two pathways, during an uneven hour. On the third day thereafter, hie to the place at same hour, and take it out: but you must not be the first person to look into the glass. It is best to let a dog or a cat take the first look into the mirror: S. Solam S. Tattler S. Echogardner Gematar.

When a Person has taken a Fatal Step how to Help and Alleviate.

Now, I step out in God's great name, now step out in his might and fame, now I step out in God's footstep, right which is against all spirits might. God the Father, before me is, God the Son behind me and at my side, God the Holy Spirit is within and with me. † † † Speak three times and move with the hand over the sore.

A Grace for Robbers and Murderers.

Be happy brethren. Brethren, thus your proud race run. We have all partaken of Christ's own blood; but ye cannot shoot me, cannot stab me, cannot flog nor punish me, because God, our Lord, will not permit it. God the Father be with thee, God the Son be with us all, God the Holy Ghost be with all of us. We will meet in joy, and part in peace. † † † Three times.

If a Person cannot Churn out.

Gilien now Punctum, Sabot Jesus of Nazareth, Holy King of the Jews. † † †

These words affix upon the stirring dish or churn.

Another for the same Purpose.

Take a card—the nine of hearts—and a knife, on which three crosses are engraved. Put these two articles under the stirring dish or churn, and all will work well.

To Fasten a Thief upon your Estate.

I, N. N. [here pronounce your name], can you pass over my estate whether you walk or ride; without the roof under the roof, if you are not able, so be you fixed to stand still, and count first all rain drops, all snow flakes, all the stars which move on the firmament, all the blades of green grass that groweth upon the earth, all grains of sand in the ocean, and all the springs that are beneath the earth. If you cannot count all these things, you shall and must stand like a log, stand like a buck, and like a goat must look. Thus, Peter, bind; St. Peter, fasten with God's own hand, and ye thieves are fastened and affixed as long as it pleases me. In his wicked position, be the thief fixed to stand, fixed to the land, and now stand still, till Judas departs from hell. Judas dare not leave the lower region; hence the thief must quiet stand still, till I may with my own eyes and hand, see and feel that wicked wight; and bid him to depart with all his might. † † † Three times spoken.

Remember where thy possessions lay, and with the right finger or hand point to them. This obey.

To release: Without trouble to thee or me, depart from hence, in the name of the Evil One, without mirth or glee.

To Regain the Stolen Property.

Take three crumbs of bread, three pinches of salt, and three very small portions of lard. Then make a strong fire, lay all these nine articles upon it, and speak these words, while remaining alone:

I lay for the thief, bread, salt and lard, upon the flame, for thy sin is hard; I lay it upon thy lung, liver and heart, that thou may feel a bitter smart. It shall come upon thee, need and dread, as it approaches a dire death. All veins shall in thy body burst, and cause thee pain and quenchless thirst; that thou shalt have no peace or rest, till all the theft thou hast returned and place it where thou hast taken the plunder, or be caught by lightning and thunder. † † † Recite three times.

When you have a Sprained Limb.

They have crucified the Saviour on the holy cross. It did not hurt him, it did not pain him. Hence thy sores and thy sprains will hurt thee not. Become well again. † † † Speak three times.

If desirous to See Miraculous Things.

Take Argentumorium and wrap it up in a rag, and write, with wolf's blood, upon parchment:

† Ada † † Aba ebe † † thanat do † Zancha Agola † Zaboha †

Whoever carries these words on his person will be honored by every one. What he asks for he will receive. If held before a lock, the same will open unto him.

When a Cow Loses her milk.

Take camphor, five cents' worth; three bits of assafœtida (or devil's dirt), three small spoonfuls of black sulphur, six spoonfuls of stove soot, a little of five-finger herb and iron herb, and milk of the troubled cow. Stir these things well together, and pour them all into a pail.

After a Cow has Lost her Milk.

If you find half of a horseshoe, put it into the milk while it boils. Take a switch of three-year-old hazelnut shrub—but they must not be bitten off, but have the knots from above. With them beat into the milk, and speak thus: I burn and beat thee, Trott and Morth, in all the devil's names, till thou unto me, N. N., (here pronounce the name of him you seek to aid), will return the milk of my cow. Assafœtida of the size of a bean, and magic balsam for five cents, put therein, and given upon a piece of bread three or four mornings in succession. In the morning early, and evening after feeding.

Another Remedy for the same Ailment.

Take the milk, water and excrements. Put it in an unglazed pot with a lid upon it, and seal it tightly, so that the fumes cannot escape. Put it upon a fire, and allow it to boil down gently. But during twenty-four hours following this boiling, you must not lend anything unless somebody asks it "for God's sake."

How to Shoot with Accuracy.

Take a needle, wherewith the gown of a corpse had been sewed, and drive it into the stock, and you will shoot accurately.

Or:

Take the entrails of a trout caught between Christmas and New Year, and put them upon a copper lid. Burn them to powder. Put it into the stock of your gun. Also in a little bag, and hang it under the right arm. You will then be able to shoot whatever you desire. If you carry the same under your left arm, you will be gay and happy.

To make One's Self Shot-Proof.

According to this formula, on the day of Peter and Paul, at vesper tide, there spring open waywort roots, of which hunters and men of the forest believe that he who carries them on his person cannot be hit or shot.

To Catch Fish.

Take valerian, or cocculus Indicus, and make small cakes thereof with flour; throw these into the deep. As soon as a fish eats thereof, it will become intoxicated, and float upon the surface.

Another:

Camphor, wheat flour, Arund Arda ololivar aa Zsz. Mix together, and it will become a salve. If you then proceed to fish, anoint your hands and shins therewith, and miracles you will experience.

To Ascertain whether a Sick Person will Die or not.

Take a piece of bread, place it before the sick one's brow, then throw it before a dog. If he eats it, the patient recovers; if he rejects it, the sick one dies.

How to cause Blind Horses to See again, and how to Remove the Cataract.

Early on Good Friday morning, dig Antemonium. Shall take! six rad Valerian, or you may also do so on any Sunday or Friday. Three of these roots cut fine, as near the eyes as you can; the other three dry and pulverize them. Then take an egg and let the white thereof run out, and put the yolk in, and add salt until the egg shell is filled. Then skillfully close it, and set it end ways upon hot ashes, till it becomes hard like a stone. Be careful not to boil it over, because it will never be good. Pulverize it, and fill with this egg the quill of a feather, and blow the contents gently into the horse's eyes. Although it pains, it will destroy the skin that grew over the eye, and make it see again. Probatum.

How to Obtain a good Memory.

Take the gall of a partridge, and with it grease the temples every month, and your memory will be like that of Mnemon.

To Drive away and Vanquish all Foes.

Whoever carries the hemlock herb, with the heart of a mole, on his person, vanquishes all his enemies, so that they will not be able to trouble him. Such a man will obtain much. When this herb is laid under the head of a sick person, the sick one, when he sings, will get well; if he cries, he will die.

To Make a Black Horse White.

Take goat's gall, and paint the horse with it, and it will turn white.

A certain way to Stop the Blood.

Take bread and leaven, and mix with brandy to a plaster, and bind with it, sores and wounds.

For a Stubborn Horse.

On Walpurgis night, thy reverence, I hope, will one enable, to curb thy temperament unstable; for zigzag courses we are wont to keep, be kind enough and gently light us up the steep.

For the day of Labor Pains. A certain Remedy. First of all write the Following in one Line upon a Paper:

A b h z P O b L 9 h b m g n
Subratum nome nex gr.

After this the patient's name in the center. Under this inscribe the following words, also † in one row:

† Ecgitar † Circabato † Bessiabato † Argon † Vigaro Tanet.

Put this into a bag of leather and sew the same up, but the seam must be on the right side.

N. B. This must be made without a knot, on thread or band, and hung up during an uneven hour.

When a Child is Attacked.

Cut three corners of a table edge from below, of every edge a chip and a grain of salt, and a bit of bread, also a little of buck's beard. All this do noiselessly, and suspend on the child's neck, with a little unbleached yarn during an uneven hour, and with these N. N. words call the child's name, viz.: This I suspend for ransom sake, in the name of God the Father, the Son, and the Holy Spirit.

To cause the Return of Stolen Goods.

Write upon two pieces of paper, the following words, and lay the one over the door, and the other under the threshold, and the thief will return on the third day and bring back the stolen articles, viz.: Abraham † bound it, Isaac † redeemed and found it, Jacob † carried it home; it is bound as tightly as steel and iron, chains and fetters. † † †

For Marasmus of Man or Beast.

Dig mouse-ear herb on St. John's-day, hang herb and roots around the neck of the afflicted, be it man or beast.

For the Toothache.

Write upon three roads with a horseshoe nail, these words: Kex, Par, Mox. ppo, in folio, and drive the nail tightly into the wall; as long as the nail remains fast, the teeth will hurt no more.

Whether a Patient Dies or Recovers.

Take his water, drop some milk of a woman, who is nursing a male child, therein; if the milk settles upon the ground, the patient dies; but if it floats above, he recovers.

To Disgust a Person who is Addicted to Gambling.

Give sow's milk to one who is addicted to gambling, and he will feel disgusted when he wishes to play.

If a Horse is Costive.

Let it take crabs' eyes, for five cents, and in fifteen minutes the cure is effected.

EGYPTIAN SECRETS.

An excellent Eyewater for Man and Beast.

When blind, and the eyes are covered with a skin, or the eyes are darkened and dim, take the eggs of red ants and put them into a small glass. Draw a water therefrom. This glass containing the eggs must be kept well corked, so that nothing may ooze out, then put the phial into dough of rye flour and bake in the oven with other bread, and when taken from the oven let cool off with the other loaves, then carefully remove the bread from the glass, so as not to break the same, and the ant eggs will prove to have turned into water. This water apply four or five times, as may be necessary, to the afflicted eye, every time one drop only. This has been tried on man and beast.

To Dry up the Water in Cases of Gouty Diseases.

Take the skull of a corpse, scrape some bone-dust off the cranium with your knife and strew into the wounds.

When a Grapevine Breaks or Warps.

Dig red raspberry roots and suspend them to the broken vine. It will cause the vine to be all right again.

To produce a Light by which a Hidden Treasure may be Found in a House.

Take incense, sulphur, pure wax and yarn, boil it and make thereof a candle, and whenever the light extinguishes there the money is concealed.

To Wean a Tippler from Drinking Wine.

Take an apple, put it into the hand of a dying man, and let the apple remain there till the person dies. If you desire the tippler to drink only half the quantity he usually takes, give him one-half of the apple to eat; but if you wish him to abstain totally from strong drinks give him the entire apple to eat. But the drunkard must not be aware of your designs.

To make a Person dislike Gambling.

Speak to an executioner, give me some wood of a whip wherewith you have beaten criminals, and flog the gambler with this upon his naked body, and never more thereafter will he gamble.

While Travelling.

Say every morning: Grant me, oh Lord, a good and pleasant hour, that all sick people may recover, and all distressed in body or mind, repose or grace may find, and guardian angel may over them hover; and all those captive and in bondage fettered: may have their conditions and troubles bettered; to all good travellers on horse or foot, we wish a safe journey joyful and good, and good women in labor and toil a safe delivery and joy.

That none may Vanquish you, and how to Open Locks.

Take the eye of a raven, lay it into an ant's hill for eight days, and you will find a little stone thereby, that stone carry with you upon your person.

For the Fever.

Take a fresh laid egg, boil it very hard, then while hot peel it, and inscribe the following words upon it:

† Aha † Mahy † Froha; then eat it hot in three bites, and after this fast.

When you have Lost your Manhood.

When you are infatuated and bewitched by a woman, so that you may not love any other, then take blood of a buck and grease your head therewith, and you will soon be all right again.

That a Horse will not be Tired.

Put links from the chain of a gallows bird, or needles of the blade of an executor's steel into your spurs.

If Something is Stolen from your House.

Inscribe over the door of the house these names, and it will be found again:

† Chamacha, † Amacha, † Amschala, † Waystcu, † Alam, † † Elast Lamach.

That Every one will Buy from you, be it what it may.

Take a twig of a whisp wherewith a person had been lashed. Make a small ring and wind red silk around it, and put it on your finger. If you wish to sell anything it will be paid for as you desire.

A Wolf's Blessing.

The Lord Jesus Christ and St. Peter, one morning travelling together, while Holy Mary proceedeth to a heather, she said: Ah, dear Lord, whence shall we hie, we will journey over hill and dale, protect therefore, dear Lord, my flock wherever it be, St. Peter takes his key and therefore closes every wolf's jaw, that they no bone no lamb may gnaw. † † † Three times.

When an Animal has broken a Bone, and its Blood Curdles.

First of all, set the fractured limb, and in case you are not near the animal take a chair or leg of a bedstead, call both the names of owner, and that of a beast, as also the broken leg of the animal. This leg must be taken on the bedstead or chair, right or left, fore or hind leg corresponding with that of the animal in your right or left hand, as the case may be, tie it and speak: Foot I heal thee in the name of God the Father, and the Son, and the Holy Ghost. Into depth of nature peer—only believe, there's a miracle here! Recite the Lord's Prayer three times, add the Creed, and three times recited. It helps.

When a Dog is bitten by a Mad Dog.

The following words shall be given to him in a drink: Cinium † Cinium † Gossium † Strassus † God † Strassus.

When a Horse has Sprained his Foot.

Take a stone from under a water-spout, and put the horse's leg upon it, and say:

I place myself upon a hard stone, I have an ailment on my leg bone which causes me much pain, be this pain black or white, grey or red, in less than three days it shall be dead. † † † Three times spoken. Probatum.

When a Horse has been Pushed and Hurt, speak these Words Noiselessly and move the Left Foot over the Sore.

Aete Bandte, to Brante bede. † † † Three times.

For Stopping the Blood.

There stood three roses upon our Saviour's grave,—the first is mild the other is good, the third shall stop thy blood, † † †. Three times.

To Cut Fortune Wand.

Proceed in the forenoon before twelve o'clock to a hazelnut shrub, which grew within one year and has two twigs, then place yourself toward the rising sun, and take the twigs in both hands and speak: I conjure thee, one summer long, hazel rod, by the power of God, by the obedience of Jesus Christ of Nazareth, God and Mary's own son, who died on the cross, and by the power of God, by the truth of God arose from the dead; God the Father, Son and Holy Ghost, who art the very truth thyself, that thou showest me where silver and gold is hidden.

A Blessing for Enemies.

This grant God the Father, God the Son, and God the Holy Spirit.

Now I will rise in the name of the Lord, and will wander in his path by his word and will beseech our Saviour Christ that he may lend me, upon this very day, three of his angels, for this I pray; the first he may protect me, the other keep me without weapon or arms, the third may keep my body from all harm and keep my soul, my blood and flesh, and keep my courage ever fresh. Whoever is stronger as Jesus Christ, he may approach and assail my flesh and blood. In the name of God the Father, the Son and the Holy Ghost. I praise thee heavenly host.

This may grant God the Father, God the Son, and God the Holy Spirit. † † †

For Decayed Lungs.

Take sparry gypsum or selenite...5	cents'	worth.
Saltpetre 5	"	"
Black Sulphur 5	"	"
Blue vitriol (copperas)..........1	"	"
Copper-water 2	"	"

mix well, and give a half teaspoonful, night and morning, to the cattle.

When you put the Yoke upon an Ox, for the Frst Time, Speak:

Ox; I lay the yoke upon thee, in the name of the Saint Franciscus, and bear it like our dearly beloved Lord Jesus Christ bore his cross. † † † Three times.

To cast Bullets wherewith to have Good Luck.

The seventeenth day in Christmas month, when this day comes in the sign of Sagittarius, or when the new moon comes on a Friday, cast your bullets, and you will be lucky.

For all Sorts of Swellings.

Take white sulphur, pound it fine, put it in good beer or wine, add one-fourth part vinegar thereto, also one-eighth olive oil, let it boil, and with this the swellings anoint.

To Extirpate Caterpillars.

Take a new broom, stand with it on the fourth corner of land or acre, and throw crosswise in the other corner in the devil's name, and say: Caterpillars clear out in the devil's name. When doing this, there must be a notch somewhere. Then throw the broom away from the land or acre, as far as you can possibly throw it. Probatum.

A Black Ointment, very Wholesome for Various Things especially for Sore Hoofs.

Take 1 pound of old lard.
" 1 pound of gunpowder.
" 1 pound of turpentine.
" 1 pound of honey.
" 1 quart of saltpetre.
" 2 ounces of white vitriol.
" 1 ounce of copperwater.
" A small glass of good wine vinegar.
" One handful of salt;

Bruise and mix, and boil well in vinegar, but prevent running over; the lard must not be added till the other articles are well boiled, then you may add the lard also warm, stir it all well together, then let it get cold. This plaster heals burns, gangrene and boils.

When Cattle Cough.

Powder wormwood, give it to the cattle with the food, or take black sulphur and laurel; make some powder thereof, and give it to the cattle with a handful of feed. It certainly helps.

For Swellings.

Oh, thou swelling! oh, thou swellings! oh, thou swellings! oh thou injured part! Now, I beseech thee, for the sake of the holy cross, whereupon Christ our Lord so meekly suffered, by our Lord Jesus' holy five wounds which never swell and never fester, and cause no gangrene and suppuration. Three times during every twenty-four hours to recite.

A Plaster for a Sore Breast.

1 quart of rosin,
1 quart of lard,
Unwatered butter,
1 quart of wax,
1 quart of linseed oil,
Saffron for five cents.

All these articles boil together, and strain through a white cloth, and let it grow cold.

When a Man has Trod on a Thorn or Briar, Glass, Etc.

Buy red lead or minium, paint the sore spot, and draw it out.

For the Flux.

Take camphor gum, venetian soap, green juniper berries, and cognac brandy; put all in a little bag and apply.

When the Lungs of Cattle Swell.

Take some sand stone, put it into a bake-oven till it becomes right hot, then put it into a pail of fresh water. Let the cattle drink thereof, and be relieved.

For the Itch or Scab.

Take precipitate, lard and white hen's manure, make a lye thereof, and wash the skin therewith.

For the Erysipelas.

God grant, God the Father, God the Son, and God the Holy Spirit. Thou wild fire I stop thee, to this end help me dear Lord Jesus Christ, that no one may be able to aid thee, wild fire flee, as his own son were he. Wild fire, I am the man who can compel thee to desist. † † † Three times.

To Stop Bleeding.

Was it not a happy hour when Jesus Christ was born, was it not a fortunate hour when Jesus Christ arose from the dead.

These three blissful hours stop thy bleeding and heal thy wounds, that they may not swell or fester, and within three or nine days be well again. † † †

When a Woman suffers from a Local Weakness.

Carraway seed oil, juniper-brandy, and juniperberry oil, of each ten cents' worth. When the pain is felt, one or two teaspoonfuls thereof to be taken.

For the Saint Anthony's Fire.

Take a piece of fox lung, and sew it in one of the patient's garments (without his knowledge), and during the remainder of his life he will be entirely free from this disease.

For Open Sores.

Take hog's lard of the size of a bean, heat it, put the yolk of an egg and some saffron therein; stir it well together. It heals.

For Swellings.

Aniseed, five cents; oil of turpentine, five cents; oil of juniper, five cents; mix and stir well. Grease the swelling therewith.

For Coagulated Blood.

Take five cents' worth of nomo, make a plaster of it, and put it upon the injury once or twice.

What Black Snails are Good for.

They exterminate warts and corns on hands and feet, heal ruptures and other injuries. They must be prepared thus: Put all the snails together in a pot, throw much salt therein, bury the pot for nine days, after this distil the matter in a glass in the sun.

Against Lockjaw of Animals.

The long finger, with three forefingers, put into the mouth, and say three times: Hefeda, Hefeda, Hefeda open, be opened. † † †

When a Person has Imbibed too much.

Take fungus of a linden tree, one-half quart of old wine, one-half quart of water, pour the latter on the fungus, let it draw for twenty-four hours, and drink mornings, noon and evenings thereof, one teaspoonful. It is a sure cure.

A Salve for Gouty Limbs.

Take dogs' lard for five cents, oil of white fir-tree cones five cents, olday for five cents, seal oil for five cents, a quart of lard, in which all the others are rendered down, and the gouty limb anointed with this salve.

Another Remedy for Gouty Limbs.

Take rabbits' lard, four ounces; brandy, two ounces; deer's marrow, nine ounces; dog's lard, nine ounces; fox lard, five ounces; juniper oil, three ounces; laurel oil, five ounces; all this well mixed, and applied while warm.

A Receipt for Man and Beast against Injuries.

Take alder tree bark, two handfuls; wormwood, two handfuls; rue, two handfuls; small sage two handfuls; garlic, two handfuls; carraway, two handfuls. Mix these all together, and fumigate stables, outhouses and other apartments therewith. It is a good disinfectant.

When Horses have the Itch.

Take one pound of gunpowder, one pound of linseed oil, one pound of carraway seed, and one pound of sulphur. Make a lye of chicken manure, pour the above substance therein, and wash the horse with this solution.

To Drive away Lice.

Fishberry and lard mixed together, and the head anointed therewith.

A Drink for Horses.

Watercresses, green juniperberries, hartshorn, venetian soap. Of these make a beverage.

A Plaster for the Worm.

Spiritus Salis, gall of glass, brown garlic, yeast, common nettle roots, honey, venetian glass, of all, three cents' worth, turpentine, whiskey, lampblack, sperm oil, swallow water. Mixed well together, and applied as plaster.

EGYPTIAN SECRETS.

When a Rifle or Shot Gun is Bewitched.

Take five cents' worth of liquid amber, assafœtida, river water, and mix well together. With the mixture clean well, and the rag, with which the scouring was done, hang up in the smoke, or put in a new-made grave.

For Dropsy.

Three flowers stand upon the grave of the Saviour Jesus Christ. The one signifies goodness of God, the other, humility, the third, God's will. Water, stand still. † † †

A Good Ointment for Wounds.

Take one-half quart of vinegar, one-half pint of honey, one ounce of verdigris, one ounce of dragon's blood, one ounce of bolus minium, two ounces mastic, one ounce incense, and three ounces oil of turpentine. All mixed well together.

To Prevent Eyes from Becoming Blind.

Take pea straw, boil it, and let the fumes fumigate the eyes. Take arum water and blue vitriol, and paint the eyes with it by using a black hen's feather. Also, take the herbs, and wipe the eyes therewith. Probatum!

A Water for all Sorts of Injuries.

Take blue vitriol, white rose water, turpentine, aquafortis, and boil together until it becomes an ointment, and then apply.

When a Woman arrives at Change of Life.

Aaron roots boiled in old wine, and of this beverage drink before breakfast, and evenings before going to bed.

For Swollen Shanks or Arms.

Take brown hartshorn spirits, some camphor spirits, three ounces opodeldoc, and with it grease the limbs.

To be Sure of Three Certain Shots per Day.

Take the heart of a whoop, hang it under the right arm whenever you fire a shot.

To Kill Powder.

Take half of a pound of gunpowder, three drachms saltpetre, three drachms camphor, three drachms chalk, one handful of juniper tree foliage. Let stand two or three days. Probatum.

How to Prevent Feeling Cold in Winter.

Take nettlewort, garlic, pour lard to it, and boil together. When hands and feet are greased with this ointment, one will not feel cold.

To Catch many Fishes.

Take rose corn and mustard grain, and the foot of a weasel. Hang them in a net, and the fish will there congregate.

When a Horse has Overleaped Himself.

Speak thus: Erese is the wound; the hour blessed and sound. Happy is the man who is able to cure this horse. † † † Three times.

An Old Drink for Horses and Cattle.

Take dragon's blood, native antimony, white rock oil, saffron, of each five cents' worth, and one egg. All of this mixed in a pint of wine and given as a drink.

When Labor is Difficult.

Give her another's milk to drink, or a parsnip which must be finely bruised; tie the same over the body, she will soon be easy and come to rest.

Yellow Jaundice of Men and Women.

Take felder roots, the middle bark, scrape it and boil it, and give every two hours, two or three tablespoonfuls for a period of six mornings and evenings.

For Felons on Men and Beasts.

† R a b h q   † H a s b a   † E b n L H
a † K a c K a a b u l a   † K a s H a S
† a † a o † b † o † † † o †

Write the above upon a scrap of paper, and put upon the sore spot.

If you Desire to Securely Shoot, put under the Barrel of your Gun, Etc., the following:

D. E W D W S H H D F S K O M W V R
V J S K N u F M U E S O Mi

To be Secure against a Shot.

O Josaphat, o Tomosath, o Plasorath; these words pronounce backward Jarot three times.

When a Person has an Open Cranium.

Lift your head upward to heaven. I view in the realms above, I view the house of God in love. It looks upon me, the Holy Trinity, who can allay my troubled head. † † †

When a Horse is Foundered.

Give iron herb (vervain) with the feed, it helps surely.

For Yellow Knots on Cattle.

Master wort,	4 ounces	Vines of rue,
Castornell wort,	4 "	Wormwood seed,
Tormentil wort,	4 "	Burnt hartshorn, 3 oz.,
Juniper berries,	4 "	Black sulphur, and

Red Antimonium.

Of all these articles make a powder, and give to old cattle from one to two ounces every morning before feeding, then let it stand for two hours and after this feed it, but give no drink before evening.

When an Animal becomes Suddenly Ill and Remains Motionless.

This is a certain indication of internal inflammation. Take two spoonfuls of fresh ashes and a half a spoonful of gunpowder, one quart of cow's milk, pour it altogether; or, make a lye of grape-vine ashes mixed with goats' milk, to measure altogether one quart. In case goats' milk cannot be obtained, take sweet oil for ten cents, and mix it with the lye. Pour it out to the animal as soon as the above indications are noticed. It will surely help.

If you have given these prescribed articles to the animal, and it becomes soon better, the head of the animal should be lifted up for the period of fifteen minutes, or tie the same, so that the blood can run toward the heart. But if the ailment is on a foot, the animal lifts the foot up and cannot stand on it, in such a case take two spoonfuls of fresh ashes, one half spoonful of black sulphur, one-half spoonful of gunpowder, and one pint of fresh cow's milk, mix this well and pour into the sick animal, thereupon take hold of the injured foot. If the skin puffs and swells and shows great heat, and also rustles, rub the leg violently toward the hoofs; then make a bandage of a flour-bag, and tie the foot tightly so that the heat or flux may not be able to extend farther upward, thereupon cut the skin open about a finger's length under the sore, and press it well, wash out with brandy, and the disease will not extend any further. Then withdraw the bandage from the foot, take fresh glue and mix it with vinegar to a plaster, and tie it upon the wound, this will draw the heat out.

Great care is to be taken that the ailment does not extend to the other feet. But should the heat extend upward, take a sharp knife and cut the skin open, that it receives air, and apply the same glue and vinegar plaster to it; or, take an iron for letting blood, and with it slit the skin whenever the disease shows itself. A poisonous steam will ooze out, and thus the animal may be kept alive. All this must be done, however, before twelve hours elapse.

For Stoppage of Water in Man or Woman.

Take rock flint stone, five cents; emetic tartar water, ten cents; crab's eye, five cents; one handful of cornellian cherries, and a small glass of brandy. All this mix well, and partake two or three times thereof. It will surely help.

An Excellent Remedy for Apoplexy.

Take a considerable portion of linden-tree blossoms and May flowers, six ounces of fresh bay leaves, bruise in a mortar to a mush. Then take a pint of blue violet sap, in this dissolve white rock candy sugar as much as will dissolve therein; pour this over the mush and mix well in the mortar. Then strain all the juice out through a cloth; wormwood salt dissolved in a half pint is added thereto and all is to be rectified in a retort, also through an alembic distil so that no phlegm remains in the mixture. Thus an excellent spirit will be obtained, which must be kept in a glass vessel hermetically sealed.

Whoever is attacked with apoplexy may take one-half teaspoonful of this spirit dissolved in linden blossom water, or other distilled water in good wine, etc. It will certainly prove a good remedy, and secure good health for future.

For Colic.

Take a handful of camomile flowers, boil them in goats' milk. Pour it out to the horse. It is a good remedy.

When a Person suffers from a heavy Fall, Etc.

Take hot ashes, six ounces filings, four ounces gold-litharge, three ounces oil of turpentine, two ounces oil of roses or olive oil.

These articles mix together, and boil till the matter becomes like an ointment, grease a piece of linen with it, and apply to the injured part.

When the Lungs and Liver of Cattle are Diseased.

Take green juniper berries and gentian and lung herbs, make powder thereof; give it a few times to the cattle. It will certainly alleviate.

When a Horse has Hair Worms.

Take ginger, pepper, chicken manure, warm cow manure and vinegar; mix together, and pour it out to the horse for a drink. Probatum.

For Swellings.

Take hempseed, wool herbs, carrots, and boil in vinegar. Make a tepid poultice thereof, and apply to the swelling, be it even near the heart. A quick relief will reward the trouble.

For Coagulated Blood in Limbs.

Take oil of dill and grease the limbs therewith. It helps.

For Proud Flesh.

Take copper water one ounce, white bees'-wax, rosin and olive oil. Pound and mix together. Apply to the flesh. It destroys the proud flesh.

For Swelled Knees.

Take hempseed, mangolt, dog's wort, pound them, add vinegar; let them boil and apply in tepid temperature. Or take honey, oakum and vinegar, boil together, and apply in poultice form.

When the Breast of a Horse is Swollen.

Take tallow from a buck as lard, saffron, tree-salt, wool oil, gunpowder, linseed oil; mix together, and apply as a plaster.

For all sorts of Breast Swellings, Heart Swellings, or Swellings of the Genital Organs of Animals.

Take skunk cabbage herb, linseed, wool herbs, red bolus; mix together, and apply as a plaster.

For the Glanders of Horses.

Take sweet oil, mercury, gunpowder and saltpetre, mix well together and pour into the nostrils of the horse, or, take the blood of a white goose, chicken manure, sweet oil, and saltpetre, put this also into the nostrils.

When a Horse has the Staggers.

Take the white of several eggs, one quart of sweet oil; mix and pour it before feeding into the horse's throat. Probatum.

For the breaking out of Felons.

Take venetian glass, pulverize it, Spanish pepper, honey and winter galls; mix together, spread it upon a stone-bear-cloth and apply to the horse's sores; let it remain for three days and the worm will ooze out.

Another Remedy for the same Ailment.

Take cooper's water, filings, verdigris, linseed oil, milano pepper. Of these make an ointment, and apply to the felon.

When it becomes Difficult to Churn.

Put the following words into the stirring dish or churn:—
Gillicum, Punctum, Satbot, Jesus Nazarenus, holy King of the Jews. † † †

An Ointment for all kinds of Wounds.

Take deer's tallow, beef's marrow, chicken fat, coal oil, sweet oil; mix all well together.

To Stop the Water in cases of Dropsy.

Take leaven from a baker, tie it around the ailing member, then burn the leaven to powder and blow into the sore.

Or: Take laurel leaves, pulverize them, and apply to the

EGYPTIAN SECRETS.

injured parts, or take the dandruff of a horse's head and put it into the wound.

Or: Powdered dog's waste.

A Good Ointment.

White rosin, five cents; linseed oil, five cents; wagon grease, three cents; two handfuls of lamp black, the white of three eggs, dust apple, and boil together.

To make a good Green Salve.

Butter, five cents;   Grease, five cents;
Balm Oil, five cents;   Verdigris, five cents;

mix together; or take ashes, lard, and anguish honey, of a like quantity, and make an ointment thereof by mixing.

A Good Ointment for Wounds.

Take a quart of firtree-harz or rosin, same quantity of wax, also of wagon grease and tallow, the same quantity. Put all of these ingredients into an unglazed pot and boil, after this mix turpentine oil with it.

To make a Splendid Horn Salve.

Take tallow, wax, grease, beef's marrow and oil of turpentine, and mix all these articles well. Or take five grains chloride of antimony, hog's lard, hoof lard, sugar honey, sheep tallow, olive oil, linseed oil, and mix all these articles together.

For a Felon.

Red bolus, two spoonfuls ground; alantis root, two spoonfuls ground; seventree, two spoonfuls ground; acorns, two spoonfuls ground; white bolus, two spoonfuls ground; white chalk, two spoonfuls ground; garlic, three spoonfuls ground; assafœtida, five cents' worth; pulverize and mix well together.

This give to a horse mornings, before feeding, in fresh water. After this burn a mole, powder it, and strew into the wound.

For old Sores which no Person could Heal.

Take sassafras and sarsaparilla for ten cents; Indian bolus and coral bolus, each for twenty cents.

For the Prolapsus.

Three women are sitting on the sands, they have intestines in their hands—of man, horse or cattle, they are—the first matron moves it, the second closes it, the third puts it in shape again. † † †

For St. Anthony's Fire for Cattle.

Inscribe upon a scrap of paper, this:

AGO, MAGO, MAGOLA.

Give it to the cattle to eat.

To Compel the Return of Stolen Goods.

Take off the left shoe, and with the left foot advance when you step out, and put manure upon the big toe, hold the left foot out. Make a fire of grape vine wood at twelve at midnight, throw the manure into the fire in the devil's name and speak. Ensuer, this I throw upon the burn, so long till the thief returns my stolen goods, as sure as God hath cast thee into the abyss of hell, when the thief returns my own, bid him leave in the devil's name. Probatum est.

The Costiveness of Horses.

Take a handful of oak lung herbs and a handful of veronica, a handful swallow roots, and a pint of water. Boil all of these; it is good for the purpose.

For Bewitched Cattle.

Sulphur, five cents; Magic balm, five cents.
Balsam, five cents; Mithridat, five cents.
Blue finherb water, five cents.

Mix these all together, and give at once to drink. Probatum. But this must be given while the cow is being milked.

A Certain Remedy for Stubborn Horses.

Native antimony, five cents; copper water, five cents; vitriol, five cents; oleum philos, five cents; half of these must be burnt; the other half dissolve in twelve quarts of water, of vitriol and copper, put half of each into the water, likewise ashes of grape vines and old shoes pulverized. Put this into the injury and wash clean with water. Repeat twice or three times per day.

For Marasmus of Children.

The child must be carried in the morning toward the rising sun, then speak: Be welcome in the name of God, thou sunshine, whence comest thou so mild, help me and my dear child. God the heavenly Father, pray, that my child help he may. Beseech the Holy Ghost, that by the heavenly host he may return the natural blood and flesh unto my child.

That no Person will Deny Anything to you.

Take a rooster, three years old, throw it into a new earthen pot, and pierce it through, then put it into an ant's hill, and let it remain until the ninth day thereafter, then take it out again and you will find in its head a white stone, which you must carry on your person, and then nobody will deny you anything.

For Lung Disease.

Pour milk in the ear.

Alum, five cents; blue vitriol, one grain; sulphur, five cents; sulphur flowers, five cents; laurel-leave flour, five cents. Take a good glassful of wine vinegar and one glassful of old wine; mix well together, and give it in the drink of the sick animal.

For an Open Head.

Now protect thy head the name of God, I looked from out the window, and beheld the mansion of God, I saw a man pure and white, who can bless thy head and grant thee blissfulness. † † †

That no Horse will get Blind.

Take quail's lard, put it in the eyes twice per day, and hang saladine herbs around its neck. Such a horse will never become blind.

For the Jaundice of Horses.

Take sour or bitter mustard, and mix with it the feed for the horse. It will recover at once.

To Stop the Blood.

Three roses upon God's acre stood—the one is called humility, the other gentleness, the third stops the blood. † † †

When a Person cannot hold his Water.

Take three pinches of egg-shell powder, of eggs from which the young chicks came out.

For Pestilence write over the Door:

1. † 2. 7, D. 1. A. † B I 2. S. A. V. † 2 †, H. 6 f. †. B. F. 2. S. † † †

For Robbers and Thieves.

I conjure thee, by the holy rose-colored blood, that thou wilt do no injury to my body or life, and to this end may God aid me. God the Father, God the Son and Holy Ghost. Gun retain thy fire and shot, as our Lord Jesus Christ was kept meekly upon the cross.

For the Fever.

Take ten cents' worth of broom kerbel, powder dry, put these into a glass of old wine, and let it stand twenty-four hours. Whenever the fever comes make two portions of the mixture, and take the greater part thereof, and eat nothing for half an hour afterward; then take the remaining part and fast for one hour.

To Discern the Thief who Robbed you.

Take the seed of sunflowers, which you must gather in the sign of the Lion in the month of August. Wrap the same up over a wolf's tooth; then take a bay leaf and wrap the tooth therein, then take the tooth, put it above your head, and you will see the thief.

For the Monkfall of Cattle.

Take one-half of a pound of blue lily rocks; three handfuls of bleached barley; one quart of wine; one half pint of water; boil all these together to a mush; divide into three parts for three drinks. Repeat every six hours. Probatum.

Another.

Obtain one half of a quart of slakening water from an apothecary, alum for five cents; mix with this water, and give it to the old cattle to drink. It helps.

When Cattle are Swelled.

Take quarter of an ounce of Dutch snuff, put it into the cattle's throat, so as it must swallow the stuff. It is a sudden cure.

To Purify the Blood.

Five cents' worth tincture of myrrh; pint of wine; mix and let it stand over night. Mornings before breakfast take a wine-glass full thereof. It helps.

A certain Remedy for the Eyes.

Take a jug which holds a pint, put waywort flowers therein. Seal it hermetically, and inter it for a period of fourteen days in a climber heep (sweepings), then take the water and wash your eyes therewith.

When a Person cannot pass Water.

Take rock-flint, burning water, crab's eyes, a handful of cornelian cherries, add a glass of brandy. Take this two or three times. It helps.

Gold Roots for the Teething of Children.

When children are teething suspend gold roots around their necks, and they will get their teeth without pain. Such root, carried on your person, secures the wearer against all harm.

Waywort heals heart woe and stomach pain. Whoever carries the roots on his person his eyes will be cured. Dog's dribbling and chacis waxes and vanes like the moon, its flowers heal those who suffers from too large a spleen or milt.

Nasturtian roots powdered, and laid upon the eyes, give clear and brilliant eyes. The sap to drink will cure liver complaint; whoever carries the root on his person will be favored by the ladies. Taken in food, it is good for cancer.

When you catch a whoop, you will find a stone, which you must put under the head of a sleeping person, and that person will be compelled to impart to you all secrets which he may know. If you carry a badger's foot with you, all your affairs will be fortunate, and you will not be perplexed, nor err.

Whoop eyes make a man benign. If you carry the eye with you you will be in good repute by the authorities; and if you will carry the head no one will cheat you.

If you carry the head of a crow upon your breast, all must love you who have dealings with you.

When you catch a mole and put it into a pot, while it lives, and ignite sulphur, all moles will gather together.

When you put a mole into an earthen pot, and boil the same, and with this water wash the hair, the hair will turn white.

During the month of August take a swallow from its nest. In its stomach you will find a stone, which you may wrap into a linen handkerchief, hang under your left arm. It is a good thing against slanderers, and makes you agreeable among the people.

A snail is said to have a starlet in its head, and when found it is good for one who is afflicted with kidney disease.

When a Person has Sprained Himself.

Take juniper berries and hay flowers, bruise them and boil in good old wine. Apply as a poultice.

For the Breaking of Felons.

Take venetian glass, half an ounce of pepper, honey, beef gall. Mix all these articles and pound them. Spread them upon a hairy cloth, and tie around the felon of the horse. Let it remain from three to four days.

For the Felons.

Give the first three scraps from the hoof of a horse which is being shod for the first time.

When a Horse has Eaten some Impure Stuff.

Take two quarts of water, put some venetian soap therein, and make a good lather. Mix for drink, warm.

Or: Take alum for five cents; cream tartar, five cents; saltpetre, five cents; red bolus, three cents; sternutative powder, two cents; Spanish pepper, stonebreak, blue vitriol, white vitriol, dragon's blood, grey sulphur, laurel leaves.

Have these ingredients mixed and pounded together. Take the first day one point of a knifeful, morning and evenings, followed by common nettle seed powdered in wine sweetened with honey. It will relieve an old cough and clears the breast, causes easy breathing and is good for cold on the lungs.

Another Cure for Dysentery.

Acron-Copaulus grind to powder, and take every morning three pinches thereof, or as much as will lay upon the point of a tableknife, three times.

Still Another.

Take a small glassful of brandy, the yolk of a fresh laid egg, and put it in the brandy. Mix the yellow well with the brandy. Give this to the patient. It helps at once.

For Gangrene, Hot or Cold.

Our Lord Jesus Christ went over the land. He blessed the cold and warm brand, that the warm brand may not burn him, and not take hold of the body till the mother of God will bear another son. † † †

For Dysentery.

Boil an egg and eat it as hot as you can, without bread or salt.

For the Water between the Skin and Flesh.

Take dog's bone, burn it to powder, and strew it into the wounds. It is a sure remedy.

When a Cow Loses her Milk.

Give to such a cow some of her own milk, or take the milk pail, and milk the cow upon the bottom of the pail, in the high name of God, and draw a cross with a knife through the milk upon the bottom of the pail, and stab into it. After this pour the milk in a running water, down the stream.

When a Horse has Worms.

Take vinegar and egg shells, chimney soot and pepper. Mix all together, give it to the horse, and the worms will all die.

When a Horse is badly Shot.

Take waywort knots, of an uneven number, and lay them upon the sore hoof.

When a Horse is Stabbed and Bleeds.

Take lard and a hot iron, and let the blood run upon it. † † †

For the Flesh Worms of Cattle.

Cut, on a Good Friday, before sunrise, alderwood, without making a noise, and make a block of it. Probatum.

For Flux, Catarrh and Sorcery.

Speak in the name of God the Father, and the Son, and the Holy Ghost.

Oh, God! I know not what has happened to you. Help thee, God the Father and our dear Lord Jesus Christ. Alas! alack! I know not what has happened to you. Help thee, God the Son, and our dear Lord Jesus Christ. Ah, God! I know not what has happened unto thee. Help thee God the Holy Ghost, and our beloved Lord Jesus Christ. With God the Father I seek thee, with God the Son I find thee, with God the Holy Ghost I drive away thy coughing, be thou palsy, vision or sorcery; be healed on this very day. Heal, heal! fast and quickly, like the fast running sun and moon, and the wind, and the fast spreading Gospel, which the Priest reads at Mass time. † † † Three times spoken.

When an Animal Loses its Usefulness.

D F W S H H D E S S Z Uz eo W V T V T D V I 1 7 F 9 W I X S V † † †

For Distempered Horses.

Take one ounce of rhubarb, antimonium, quarter ounce black snuff. Pour this three or four times into the nostrils, but mix it first in a glassful of wine and vinegar.

For Bewitched Cattle.

Take five cents' worth of sulphur balsam, five cents' worth of magic balsam, five cents' worth of mithridat, and five cents' worth of blue tin herb water. Mix well in their own milk. Probatum.

To Cure the Headache.

Take carrot-sap, and inhale it through the nose, and your aching head will be cured at once.

EGYPTIAN SECRETS.

An Old Drink for Horses and Cattle.

Five cents' worth of dragon's blood, five cents' worth of antimony, five cents' worth of white rock oil, five cents' worth of saffron, and one egg. All poured together in a pint of wine.

An Amulet for the Colic.

S † a † t † o † r, A † r † e † p † o †
T † e † n † e † t, O † p † e † r † a †
R † o † t † a s

When a Woman cannot Bear Easy.

Inscribe upon a wooden plate the above amulet, then wash it off with wine, and give it to the woman to drink.

To Heal Burns.

Take linseed oil and wax, of one as much as of the other, and render in a pan together. Paint the sore with a feather, mornings and evenings. Probatum.

For the Cattle.

With God the Father I seek thee, with God the Son I find thee, with God the Holy Ghost I drive thee away. † † †

To Heal Injuries on Man, Cattle or Horse.

Cut down a burdock bush, and put it into your house, so that it may wither. Then take a thread from a reel which had never been washed, and speak: Burdock bush, I bind thee that thou shalt heal the injury of this man (or beast, as the case may be), be it boils, sores, gout, swellings, or whatever it may be. Double the thread, and move around the bush, where the thickest part is, in the name of God the Father, and make a knot, then repeat the same in the name of God the Son, and make another knot, and repeat the same motion, while saying in the name of the Holy Spirit, and again make a knot, and say then: What I and thou cannot heal, that may heal the Holy Trinity. After this, put the bush in a place where no air moves, and the injury will be healed from the root. Probatum.

To Make Yourself Invisible.

Pierce the right eye of a bat, and carry it with you, and you will be invisible.

For the Founder of a Horse.

Let such an afflicted horse drink the water wherein a gown was washed, and which she wore during the time of her illness, and the ailment will soon vanish.

To Quench a Fire.

Run three times around the fire, and say: Fire, thou hot flame, Christ the worthy man rules thee. Thou fire, stand still. It is my will. Do not spread out any further. In the name of God the Father, God the Son, and God the Holy Spirit. Amen.

When you Hear Something said, that you may not Forget it.

Take the heart of a swallow, boil it in milk, and carry it on your person, and you will remember all you hear.

When Cattle have Soft Feet.

Take five cents' worth of aquafortis, fifteen cents' worth of brandy, three or four eggs, and put all into a dish, and let it remain a while. It will cook itself. With this grease the hoofs every day two or three times.

When Cattle are Costive.

Cut soap into five pieces, put them into a pint of milk, warm it, and give it to the cattle twice. It is a sure remedy.

When a Sore on a Horse Breaks Open.

Take laurel leaves, grind them to powder, put them into the sore, and tie it with hemp oakum.

To Still the Wild Water.

Take an apple of a hawthorn bush, let it dry, pulverize it, put it into the boil, and it will cease at once.

For Shooting Pains.

Carry upon your body:
ARILL. AT. GOLL. GOTTZO.

For Bewitched Cattle.

Take retting mugwort (artemisia on the evening of the day of Philippi and Jacobi,) and put over the door where the cattle go in and out, and no cattle can be bewitched. Probatum.

For Suppurating Limbs (Sweeny) on Man or Beast.

Suppuration and foul matter, I forbid thee the blood of my cattle, (or of human beings), the blood and flesh, marrow and bone, in the name of Jesus Christ, in the name of God the Father, the Son and the Holy Ghost. Toward the rising sun, three Fridays in succession, and before the rising of the same, also three succeeding Fridays, this must be done, always rubbing, with both hands from above downward. Always to repeat three times, and always to recite three Lord Prayers and three Creeds. Probatum.

When the Teeth of Cattle are getting Soft.

Take a handful of mush meal, put it upon the lid of an earthen pot, let it get hot, and then rub the teeth of the cattle therewith. Probatum.

For the Sprains of Cattle.

Call the cattle by name and speak: Hast thou sprained, wrenched, or overstepped thyself, the sprains or oversteppings shall never hurt you, Our Lord Jesus was innocently crucified, and it did not hurt him, so the sprains and wrenched limbs will never hurt thee in the least. † † †

That nothing Serious may ever Happen to Cattle during the Entire Year.

During Good Friday night between the hours of eleven and twelve, you must rub every animal, cattle or horse, etc., over the back, and stroke with your right hand in the three highest names, three times, and speak; This I do unto thee for boils and tumors, wild blood, griping pains and colic, and for all ailments and injuries, and for all bad people who by night will plague thee. † † † Then you must cut a cross on the tail of the cattle, and also make a little incision on both points of the ears, thus nothing serious will happen during the entire year.

Take bay leaves five cents, for five cents arrow root, engian, linden tree fungus, larch tree fungus, pepper, assafœtida, one load of gunpowder and a nutmeg, all dissolved in one quart of wine, to be taken as hot as possible.

To Heal Swellings.

Bruise common nettles, such as have a white blossom, tie these over the sores, and the swelling will vanish. This remedy is also good when the boils are accompanied by erysipelas.

For Horny Excrescences or Spavin.

Take mustard flour, make a plaster thereof by mixing it with saliva. Apply to the injury three mornings in succession.

To make the Hair Grow wherever you Chose.

Take dog's milk and paint the spot therewith, wherever you wish to have the hair grow. It will surely grow.

To Extirpate a Tumor and Abscess.

Proceed to the place where carrions are placed, and obtain a piece of an old bone, with it rub the tumor, then bury this bone under the spout of the roof, where neither sun nor moon shines or darts any rays. The ailment will vanish.

For a Swollen Foot of a Horse.

Take potter's remnants and powder made from an old shoe, also a handful of salt, and good vinegar; stir it all together, paint the foot all over, and the swelling will vanish.

For the Killing of Hoof Worms in Cattle.

Christ the Lord journeyed over the acre, upon Joseph's acre; he opens three furrows, he caught three worms; the first was white, the other was black, and third was dead and herewith N. N., all thy worms are dead. † † † Three times.

For the Erysipelas of Cattle.

Prepare a good wine soup, therein scrape two nutmegs. Let the cattle drink this. The disease will disappear.

For Rotten Lungs of Cattle.

Arrow root, five cents; saltpetre, five cents; red bolus, three cents; sternutative powder, one cent; blue vitriol, three cents; dragon's blood, five cents; laurel leaves, three cents; verdigris, three cents; cream a tartar, two cents; Spanish pepper, two cents; chipped stone, one cent; white vitriol, three cents; mix all together and pulverize. Mix with a little wine vinegar, and put a small quantity into the nostrils of the sick cattle.

For Swollen Udder.

Three matrons traveled over Mount Sinai, the first spake: My cow has swelled teats; the other said: It may be; the third spake: It be so, or it is so; so help her the name Jesus Christ. † † † Three times.

For the Inflammation of Cattle.

When cattle remain still in one place without moving, this is a sign of inward burning fever. Take native sulphur, white chalk, and gunpowder, grind it to a fine powder. Take of these ingredients half a spoonful, also a fresh laid egg; mix all these articles with fresh vinegar, and pour out to the cattle for a drink. After this tie the cow's head up for a quarter of an hour. It surely helps, and the cow will recover.

For Shrubby Feet of Horses.

Take wheaten flour, boil it to a mush, then render pitch into it, as much as you deem necessary. Thereof make a plaster, put it upon a strong cloth, wrap it around the foot, let it remain for three days, after this tear it off; and the bristles will hang to the plaster. But the hair must before this procedure be nicely cut off, then take the gown of a female, wash it, wet a cloth therein and lay it upon the horse's foot.

A Wholesome Powder which Heals all sorts of Injuries Quickly.

Take wormwood and fern leaves, also the roots of these, of the latter double the quantity, bruise the herbs and mix them together, also add powdered sugar, and take lees or dregs of wine as they come from the barrel; all these articles mix and put into a new earthen pot, which must be well closed and sealed up, to prevent evaporation. Expose the pot to a quick fire until the contents turn to a powder. This powder use for the injured spots or parts. It will certainly help.

To Heal up Wounds.

An herb called buckwheat corn, has long stems, the root thereof is white as snow, resembling a fine hair. Take this herb, and boil with the root and stem in wine and water. and paint the wounds therewith. Probatum.

A Blessing for All.

God has created water and wine, that ailments and injuries may be cured inwardly and outwardly, like Lamas pierced Christ's right side. Thus the injury may not bleed, fester nor swell. † † †

To Heal Open Sores.

Egypsiatum is a balm of much efficacy. For proud flesh, use vitriol upon the sores, this will eat the flesh up.

For Flush and Rush of Blood.

Oh, thou wild accursed flush and rush, thou hast already raged in this blood and flesh, now vanish from this flesh and blood, in the name of the Father, the Son, and the Holy Spirit. One glassful of vinegar for five cents, pepper for two cents, and a little saffron added thereto, is an excellent remedy.

When Cattle have Broken or Sprained Limbs—How to Cure them without having seen the Injury.

Call the name of cattle and that of its owner, and proceed to a chair or bedstead, and take the foot, front or rear, right or left, into both of your hands and speak: I heal thee in the name of God the Father, and the Son, and the Holy Spirit, who believes in skill of science still, it heals as fast at his own will. † † † Three Lord's Prayers and three Creeds, recited three times in succession. Probatum.

For the Colic, if we only Know the Name of the Patient.

A horn of a deer, a piece of a bread crust, a glass of red wine. These three pieces, N. N., shall be for thy colic and womb. Womb so good, womb God's blood, womb return into thy place, womb return with all good grace, or thy flesh and blood wilt enter the grave. † † †

To Prevent the Milk from being Taken from a Cow.

When a cow has calved, press a whole egg into her throat, and during this same year no one can take her milk clandestinely.

EGYPTIAN SECRETS.

When a Man has Power and cannot Urinate.

Beg for a sow's bladder, for God's sake, and fill it with soft rain-water. Then tie the bladder tight, and hang it in the smoke, and drink one teaspoonful, four times a day.

When Cattle are Swelling Up.

Take a woman's gown, and tie the cattle therewith. Probatum.

When a Cow Loses the Butter Stuff, how to Help Her.

Put these words under the churn, as follows:

    Ellieue X Lu m Z u n d w v Meillum X
    Lume Z im s v E v X eill im X Luie Z
    un d v s r x.

This is also applicable when a cow has borne a calf. Give her the same words to swallow; and when she has the fever, hang the letters round her neck, on a Friday, between the hours of 11 and 12, and let her take, three days in succession, such a letter, before eating anything else, in the morning at an uneven hour. Repeat eight days in succession. Probatum.

For Poisonous Air and Pestilence.

To suspend on man or beast, on a Friday, before sunrise, at an uneven hour, the following:

    S A T O R
    A R E P O
    T E N E T
    O P E R A
    R O T A S

† J † C † S † H S b y 1 S a n n e t.
U S M m a t e r o n n y † S b a b e 2
S †

For Hydrophobia.

Inscribe upon a loaf of bread, on the upper crust, the following words, and give it to either man or beast to eat, as the case may require:

    Gerum, Heaium Lada Frium, hide thyself.

To Exterminate a Tumor or Excrescence.

Take five cents' worth of yew salve, five cents' worth of Zillo, five cents' worth of lard, five cents' worth of laurel oil, and make an ointment thereof. Smear upon a strip of linen, and apply externally.

When Cattle cannot Pass Urine.

Take some iron herb water and cornelian cherries. If this does not relieve, take five cents' worth of dragon's blood, and let it be drank.

For all Sorts of Spots or Blisters on the Eyes.

Pronounce the following sentence three times, and blow three times over the eyes, while pronouncing the three highest names:

Our dear Lord Jesus Christ breaks skin and blisters by his holy breath, which emanated from his holy sides, while on the cross he was placed. † † †

For the Windgalls in Horses.

Take three ounces of rendered lard, one ounce of laurel oil, and one ounce of powdered Spanish fly. Pound these articles, put them into a tin box, clip the hair carefully from the galls, and put the plaster carefully thereon. Tie the horse until the gall runs out, so that the horse cannot tear it open with his teeth. Apply mornings and evenings.

How to Heal the Same.

Take two parts of wine and one part of sweet oil. Boil well, and heal the horse's wounds, after using the above remedy.

For Jaundice.

Take black hellebore, hazel roots, enzian, four ounces of each, and make a powder thereof, and give, mornings and evenings, a teaspoonful of it.

For Diarrhœa.

Take of coxcomb three parts, horse-bone two parts, two parts of shoe-sole, powder all this and mix together, and give thereof two spoonfuls morning and evening.

When Cattle have Drank too Fast after being Overheated.

Take of mitriat three pinches, pulverized juniperberries one ounce, laurel oil half an ounce, sixteen drops of prunus virginæ; mix in a pint of warm wine, and drench the cattle therewith.

For the Wind Colic.

Take water, perhaps half a pint; powdered masterwort, three drachms; olive peels and laurel oil, of each one drachm; and mix some goat's milk therewith, with a little soap and salt into the horse's fundament. Tie the horse up so that it cannot lay down.

For Diarrhœa.

Take of tormentilwort and wallwort of each two ounces, mix three pomegranates and two ounces of orange peels, bay leaves, mastix, of each one ounce. Of these articles make a powder and give a spoonful evenings and mornings mixed with the food, when it is wet.

To Heal Injuries.

Speak: Itum, Otum, Utum. Three times. † † †

For Yellow Jaundice.

Recite three times: Water do not flow, be it then that thou wilt offer me to grow and repeat seven and seventy-seven times the blow. † † †

Another Remedy for the same Ailment.

Buy aniseed for six cents of an apothecary; let from twelve to fifteen drops thereof be dissolved in a spoonful of brandy, and take inwardly two or three times per day. The jaundice will thus be cured within a few days.

For all sorts of Sorcery of Man and Beast.

The appended formula suspend upon man or beast, which may have been bewitched, during an uneven hour.

```
       † I N † R I †
          S A T O R
          A R E P O
          T E N E T
          O P E R A
          R O T A S
       C † M † B †
```

And then proceed at once up into your house, cut or file on

the spars so that it becomes like flour, and take three pinches of wheat flour and of salt. Give all of these articles mixed, to the person or cattle in the three highest name. The bad man will appear!

For Milk Thieves.

Take an apron and spread it with calves' blood, put such apron upon the back of the cow for several days, and when it has become dry, repeat as before. Repeat this three times, and the witch will smell so much of this that no one can bear to remain in her presence, and the witch will come and beseech of you to stop the smearing. When putting the blood on the first time, close the house well, that no one may enter, then sweep the room backward, put the sweepings into a black apron, lay it upon the kitchen step, and strike upon it with a hammer, and thus you will sweep the witch.

That the Use of a Cow may not be Taken.

Take camphor, eggs and black carraway, give it to the cattle and keep it in use.

If you know that the animal is taken, take all the milk from the udder, then spit into it three times, stir the milk and the former usefulness of the cow returns.

If a cow gives blood with the milk, give it to her to drink, and she will cease to give blood.

After a young cow calves for the first time, give her a piece of rock salt, and thus will obtain a healthy cow, and of such a cow the use cannot be taken.

To Prevent Bees from Flying Away.

Take the root of a blue lily, put it into the bee hive. Probatum.

An Ointment for Burns.

Take one pound of glue lard, render it down in an earthen dish, pour one-quater of a pound of linseed oil to it, mix it well till it becomes cold. If you desire to improve this, add four ounces of the liquid storax thereto, which will give it a bitter taste. With this mixture all burns and injuries caused by inward heat may be cured; also flesh wounds and mortifications. During daytime paint the injured part over twice.

The glue lard you can obtain from almost any currier or tanner.

How to make Ants' Oil and what it is Good for.

It is so valuable for the eyes and ears, that it can hardly be described. Put a lot of ants' eggs into a pot. Wrap it up in a loaf of bread, and afterward distil it in a glass by exposing it to the sun.

Thou asketh: How do we obtain the ant eggs from an ants' hill? Sweep a place clean near such a hill, put green briars or twigs thereon, stir with a stick into the hill, and the ants will carry all their eggs under the twigs or briars.

I will prove unto thee, where to obtain the incense. See after St. James's Day in the ants' hills, you will then find pieces with rosin or pitch. This is incense. Removest thou such a hill, thou wilt find holes thereunder where incense is stored away in plenty.

For Toothache.

When a person is troubled with toothache, the teeth are decayed and hollow, take cornelian cherries and wax, make little cakes thereof, and put them upon a heated iron, cover them over with a pot, which has a hole in the bottom, let the vapors rise through a funnel into the mouth, and the worms will fall out of the teeth.

For Asthma.

When a person suffers from asthma, and has a heavy breath, procure of an apothecary morsell willy file, and eat thereof, mornings early.

Take skin nettles, cut them fine, pour brandy over it, also rose leaves. Take inwardly morning and evening.

For Freckles.

When persons have freckles, catch the dew that settles on wheat, mix with rose-water and oil of lilies. With this water wash the face. It drives all the freckles away, and adds to the beauty of the face by improving the complexion.

A Cure for a Hard Disease.

Drink the milk of a young sow, having pigs for the first time. It helps.

For Consumption.

When consumption has taken hold of a person, let him take a good glass of wine in the evening. The first water such a sick person passes after drinking such wine, let run out but the second and third time put the water in a glass vessel Let this stand in a cellar for twenty-four hours till it clears Thereupon take a good portion of loaf sugar and melt the same in a copper pan. Of the water pour as much as is pure and clear into the melted sugar, and let it boil up like a soup. Rub the chest morning and evening with a wineglass full thereof. It will also cure the gravel of the bladder.

Another Remedy for Consumption.

One of the main cures for healing consumption is the following: Take lung herbs, liver herbs, (mandragora and May apple,) scrape it fine, put virgin honey and a little wine to it. Let it dry over the fire. Morning and evening as much powder thereof taken as will cover the point of a table knife. It helps.

For Neuralgia and Arthritis.

When a person has neuralgia in the limbs, also palsy and is deformed, catch an ant hill in a bag. Boil the same and wrap very warm round the limbs. Grease also with rain-worm oil.

To Cure Discharges.

Take one ounce of amber oil in four portions inwardly. Make an ointment of burnt alum, house-leek and white lilies, and diligently anoint therewith.

How discharges are cured in Vienna by Saint Marx. The patient must have a clean room, which is debarred of all fresh air; near the room must be situated a small bath-room, wherein the patient may be enabled to take a sweat bath. Give to the patient venetian mithridat. Heat brickstones and put them into the bath-room and pour water thereon. This will cause the patient to perspire and sweat the disease out.

The following must be the beverage for the patient, viz.: Take one pound of unslaked lime, pour eight quarts of water upon it. Let it stand over night, then draw the water off,

EGYPTIAN SECRETS. 129

and mix therein two ounces sassafras, two ounces sarsaparilla, two ounces licorice root, one drachm saffron, two ounces rock candy. This pour into the wounds and sores. Take also the earth which ants carry upon the sod.

For Chiragra or Gout.

When a person feels that he will be smitten with the gout, he must take hold of an ant hill and put the same into a bag; cook it and poultice very hot, and thus frighten the disease away.

For Matter Discharges.

Take the excrementis of a gander and tie it warm over the organ.

To Prevent Witches from entering a Stable.

Take white elfencoop wood, make plugs therefrom, and drive them into all the doors and thresholds of the stable, and no witch can enter. If a witch is already in the house, it cannot leave.

When the Milk of a Cow is Taken.

Take a new cover of a pot, which has never been used. Make it red hot. Take a dish whereon this lid will fit. Then put a dish over it, and milk bravely, while the cover yet glows red, and it will boil and come to pass that the witch will be covered all over with spots. Then pour the milk into the dish, and cover it that nothing can get to it. But prior to this, let the cattle take the following characters:

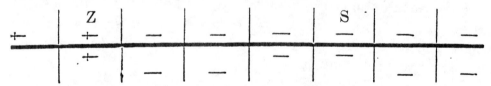

M W st O E V F E L S D K E C K 34 W E † R A U E X X.

A. M. E. R. A. Sator Arepo Tenet Opera Rotas Hagobeas Agablet gricherma alle maas nastia Helenfasz Marablium. Make three crosses with black carraway seed oil upon the other side of the paper, and with holy oil.

That a Horse may not become Stiff or Founder.

Pliny writes: Hang a large wolf's tooth around its neck.

When a Horse has eaten Feathers.

Take the stomach of a hen and give it to the horse to eat.

To make a Blind Horse See again. (From a Turkish Horse Doctor.)

Take a fish called asche, and make an oil of it, which is done in the following manner: procure a new earthen pot, holding half a quart, and put it upon another pot holding but a pint. These inter so that they keep on top of each other, and the one above stands over, and projecting above the ground. Seal hermetically so that no air can get in; but in the bottom must be five holes, so as to permit the oil to run into the lower pot. The fish must be placed in the upper pot. Around the upper pot make a fire, and the fish will melt, and the oil will flow into the lower vessel. Take this oil, and grease the horse's eyes therewith frequently during the day. In the course of four weeks horses so treated will see again.

To Drive the Worms from the Corn.

If the worms come into the corn, take oilberry wood, burn it to powder, strew such powder over the corn and all the worms must die.

To Remove Itch and Lice from Cattle.

Proceed to a place where the oaks have been cleared, and upon the stumps, after a rain, you will find a yellow water. Take a quart of this water, which you may gather with a clean sponge or cloth, and pour to it a pint of herring sauce, such as remains in a cask or keg after the last fish has been taken out. All this mix, and with this liquid wash the places where the cattle are lousy or have the itch. Thus lice and itch are banished visibly.

When a Cow Loses her Milk.

In such a case, let the cow drink her own milk, mornings before feeding, and the milk will return.

When a Person or Cattle have been bitten by a Poisonous Animal or have been Poisoned.

Catch a large toad on the thirtieth of a month, during the two days of the moon's period. Spear this toad and let it dry in the sun. On whatever is poisoned, lay this dry toad. It reduces the swelling and draws the poison out. It is also good in time of pestilence. Every housekeeper should supply herself with such a toad. It will do her good.

For a Weak and Dull Head.

When a person has a weak head and is often absent-minded, take hold of an ant's hill, put them into a bag, boil the same for six hours in a kettle of water. Draw this water upon bottles and distil it in the sun. With such water wash the weak and dull head. If the disease is very bad, bathe the patient in such water. The blood of asses should also be drank.

To Drive the Mice away from Barns.

Burn a rotten crab to powder, fumigate the barns with it and all the mice therein will die.

For Ruptured Children.

An approved powder, by the grace of God, for a child having been ruptured. It has helped many a person already. Take black and white roots of crowfoot, scrape them clean and grind them fine, sift through a sieve. Give every morning before breakfast, in a spoon, while the moon is waning. To an infant only three pinches thereof. Can also be used with advantage by grown persons.

To Gild Tin, Glass or Leather.

Take four pounds of linseed oil, boil it in a glazed earthen pot, so long till a feather dipped therein burns up; then mix sixteen ounces of varnish and eight ounces of aloes therewith. Stir all well together and boil till it obtains the thickness of a syrup. Should the color be too light, mix from three to four ounces aloes thereto, and less varnish, and the color will be a shade darker and nearer the gold color. After this color has boiled sufficiently long, take it off the fire so that the flame may not touch it, otherwise it will all burn up. Save it, the older it is, the better it will be. If you desire now to gild tin or glass, paint with a paint brush and it will resemble the color of gold.

Truthful Prognostics from Egypt, found in the Library of Dr. Plein Horatio, Astronomer of the Khedive of Egypt: as follows:

Whereas, forty-two days of an entire year are unfortunate days, according to a Greek author, he who gets sick on one of these days mentioned hereafter, will not easily recover, viz.:—

The 1, 2, 6, 11, 17, 18..................January
The 8, 16, 17.........................February
The 1, 12, 12, 15.........................March
The 3, 15, 17, 18..........................April
The 8, 10, 17, 30...........................May
The 1, 7, 10...............................June
The 1, 5, 6................................July
The 1, 3, 18, 20.........................August
The 15, 18, 30........................September
The 15, 17.............................October
The 1, 7, 11..........................November
The 1, 7, 11..........................December

Hereby is to be noted:

1. A child born on such a day will not live long, and if it lives, it will be of poor health and vigor.

2. If persons marry on any of these days, they will be apt to separate, and live in quarrel and poverty.

3. If a person commences a voyage on such a day, he will generally return home sick, or meet with an accident in body or goods.

4. On such days do not commence to build, sell no young cattle, nor sow or plant anything. Do what you may, it will all come to trouble.

5. During these mentioned forty-two days, five days are especially unlucky days, on which no journey should be taken, namely: The 3d of March, the 17th of August, the 1st, 2d and 30th of September. To this must be again noted thereof, three days are especially unlucky days, and any man shedding blood on such a day will surely die within seven or eight days thereafter, as namely:

The 1st of April, on which Judas the traitor was born.

The 1st of August the devil was rejected from heaven.

The first of December Sodom and Gomorrha was destroyed.

Whoever is born on any of these unhappy days, he will die of a violent death, or will be disgraced before the world, and seldom reaches old ages.

A Remedy for Restless Persons.

The water of the herb called hen-bane, is good for those who have unnatural restiveness. The head should often be bathed therewith, or cloth soaked in this water, and laid on the temple, will restore natural rest and sleep.

When a Cow Loses her Use, how to Mark the Witch.

Milk such a cow on a Friday morning before sunrise. Take the milk-pail, turn it over, and milk over the bottom of the pail two, three or four times, until you obtain a few pots of milk. Then you will also have to procure nine small pieces of wood, which you must either steal or beg for God's sake, but you may return them afterward. Then make a fire, take an iron pan, wherein boil the milk, in which put three tufts of hair of the cow, one from between the horns, one from the shoulder-bone, one from the loins. Thereafter take a handful of salt and a half handful of chimney soot. Now take three, spades or three scythes, heat them in fire and temper them off in the milk, turn them crosswise therein. Then take a hog's bladder, put the milk therein, and hang in the smoke.

If this does not help, write the characters upon spade or scythes as follows:—B. D.

INDEX TO VOL. II.

Agreeable to all, how to make one's self.................. 76
Ambrose Stone 77
Ant's Oil, how to make....................................127
Apoplexy, an excellent remedy for........................106
Approved representation 77
Asthma 127
Banishment, a 70
Bear easy, when a woman cannot...........................117
Bed Bugs, to drive away...............................74, 77
Bees from flying away, to prevent........................126
Bewitched Cattle 110, 116
Birds, to understand the song of.......................... 74
Black horse, to make it white............................. 93
Black Ointment, wholesome for various things............. 98
Black Snails, what they are good for.....................101
Bleeding of a Wound, to stop..........................68, 74
Blessing for All..122
Blessing for Enemies...................................... 98
Blind Horses to see again.............................92, 130
Blister, to make.. 68
Blood of Patients, how to stop........................74, 97
Blood, to purify the......................................113
Blood, to stop the, of one whose name is only known...... 77
Boils and Swelling.. 86
Boils on the Hoof, to heal................................ 67
Breast Swellings, Heart Swellings, etc...................108
Broken Bone, and when the blood curdles.................. 97
Bullets to cast, wherewith to have good luck............. 99
Burns, to make an ointment for........................67, 77
Butter Stuff, when a Cow loses her.......................123
Buy, that everybody will, from you........................ 96
Caterpillars, to destroy.................................. 99
Cattle, are costive....................................... 85
Cattle, cannot pass water.................................124
Cattle, for the swelling of...........................67, 113
Cattle, yellow knots in...................................105
Chicken Pox 72
Child is bewitched, when a................................ 79
Child, when a woman cannot give birth to a...............117
Churn, when it becomes difficult to......................108
Churning of butter, if a person cannot churn out.........108
Colic 81, 84, 107, 117
Coagulated Blood 89, 101
Consumption 128

134

INDEX TO VOLUME II.

Costiveness of Cows..................................81, 85
Costiveness of Horses................................77, 94
Cough of Cattle... 98
Cow losing her milk..........................86, 91, 115
Cow, having calved, to prevent her milk being taken during
  year 81
Decayed Lungs 98
Diarrhœa 124
Distempered Horses 116
Dog, horse or other animal to run after you, to compel.... 73
Drink for Horses..................................102, 117
Dropsy 103
Dysentery, two cures for..............................115
Erysipelas 79, 100
Escape, to present a person to......................... 73
Eye, cataract of the................................... 67
Eyes, spots in the..................................... 67
Eye-water, excellent 95
Eyes, certain remedy for the....................103, 113
Fall, when a person suffers from a....................107
Felons of men and beasts..................104, 108, 114
Fever 67, 96
Fish, to catch... 92
Flush and Rush of Blood...............................122
Flux, for the 100
Foes, to drive away all................................ 93
Fortune's Wand, to cut a.............................. 98
Founder, that a horse may never get stiff or..........118
Foundered, when a horse is............................105
Fractured Legs and Open Sores......................... 82
Freckles 127
Frosted Feet 87
Gambling, to disgust a person against...............94, 95
Gangrene, hot or cold.................................115
Glanders of a Horse...................................108
Gold Roots for the teething of Children...............113
Gout and Sweeny..................................86, 102
Gravel 85
Grape Vine, when it breaks or warps................... 95
Green Salve, etc. (the celebrated genuine)............109
Gun, to prevent a person from firing a................ 73
Hair, to grow wherever you choose, how to make........120
Hair Worm 85
Hard Disease, cure for a..............................127
Hares from destroying Cabbage, how to prevent.........
Headache 116
Heel Injuries 121
Herb Wine 86

INDEX TO VOLUME II.

Hidden Treasures, how to be found...... 95
Horse is Sick, or has the Blind Fistula, when a...... 69
Horse is Swollen, when the Breast of a...... 108
Horse refuses to be Shod...... 87
Horse Salve, or Horse Ointment...... 109
Horse that cannot stall...... 73
Horse that will not get Tired...... 96
Horse, when it has been pushed and hurt...... 115
Horses and Cattle, an old drink for...... 102
Hydrophobia 123
Intended wife to love you, how to cause...... 76
Inflammation of Cattle...... 121
Influenza, Toothache, Headache...... 70
Illicit Love, a magic for one who is infatuated by...... 70
Injuries, a water for all sorts of...... 103
Injuries of man or beast...... 117
Invisible things, how to discern...... 75
Invisible, how to make yourself...... 117
Imbibed, when a person has too much, is dead drunk...... 101
Impure stuff, when a Horse has eaten some...... 114
Itch of Horses...... 102
Itch or Scab 100
Jaundice of Horses...... 104
Labor Pains 93, 104
Lame Limbs 85
Lice, to drive away...... 102
Lockjaw of Animals...... 101
Locks to Open...... 74
Lung and Liver of Cattle, diseased...... 100, 107
Lung Disease 84
Mad Dog, when bitten by a...... 97
Man, Cattle or Horses, to heal injuries on...... 102
Mange or Itch of Sheep...... 72
Manhood, when you have lost your...... 96
Marasmus 94, 111
Memory, to obtain a good...... 93
Measles in Children...... 85
Mice, to drive away...... 131
Milk from being taken from a cow, to prevent...... 122
Milk Thieves 126
Mirror, to make a, in which everything may be discerned...... 89
Moles from their holes, to draw...... 73, 83
Money, how to obtain...... 74
Monkfall of Cattle...... 112
Neuralgic Pains or flush of man and beast...... 84
Ointment, a good for any purpose...... 103
Open Cranium, when a person has a...... 105
Open Head 111

INDEX TO VOLUME II.

Open Sores 101
Ox, how to put the Yoke the first time upon............. 98
Pains, how to allay.. 81
Palsy 85
Patient, whether he Dies or Recovers....................... 94
Person, if chaste, how to try.. 76
Person will deny you anything, that no..................... 86
Pestilence 112
Plaster for the Worm... 102
Playing, how to have good luck in............................. 76
Poisonous Air and Pestilence...................................... 123
Powder, a wholesome... 121
Powder, to kill... 103
Prevent anybody from taking anything belonging to you.. 87
Proud Flesh 107
Purchase cheaply, and sell at high prices................. 74
Rabid Dogs, for bites of.. 75
Rider or several horsemen, to stay............................ 70
Rifles or Muskets to miss fire, to cause.................... 72
Robbers and Murderers 89, 112
Rotten Lungs of Cattle... 120
Rupture 72
Ruptured Children 131
Salt Rheum 88
Scythes for Mowing, to sharpen.................................. 74
See miraculous things.. 91
See, if a Person is Chaste... 76
See what others cannot see... 73
Sheep, for the purging of... 72
Shoot, to shoot with accuracy...............................91, 104
Shooting Pains 92
Shotgun is bewitched, when a.................................... 103
Shotproof, to make One's Self...............................73, 75
Shots per day, to be sure of Three............................. 103
Shrubby feet of horses... 121
Sick Persons, to ascertain whether they will Live or Die.. 92
Soft Feet, when Cattle have.. 118
Sorcery 116
Sore Feet 79
Sore on Horse breaks open, when a........................... 122
Spavin 93
Sprains 97, 114
Sores, which no Person can Heal................................ 109
Spirits, to lay, by anathema.. 71
Sprained Limb 90
St. Anthony's Fire...101, 110
Staggers, when a Horse has the................................. 108
Stirring Butter 88

INDEX TO VOLUME II.

Stolen Property, to cause the return of..71, 73, 78, 79, 90, 94
Stomach, Drops 87
Stoppage of Water in Man or Woman.....................106
Stubborn Horses 93, 110
Stupid, when an Animal is................................ 83
Suddenly ill when an animal becomes..................... 82
Suppurating Limbs 113
Sweetheart shall not Deny you........................... 76
Swellings of every kind........................79, 100, 107
Target, to prevent a person from hitting the............ 72
Teeth of Cattle are getting soft........................119
Theft, in case one suffers from......................... 68
Thief, to fix a......................................88, 89
Tin, Glass or Leather, to gild..........................131
Tippler, to wean a Drunkard from drinking............... 95
Toothache 71, 94
Transfix a Rider.. 88
Traveling, a charm while................................ 96
Truthful Prognostics 132
Tumor or Abscess, to extirpate..........................120
Usefulness, when an animal loses its...................116
Use of a Cow may not be taken, that the................126
Vanquish, that no one may vanquish you, and how to open
    locks 96
Water in cases of Dropsy................................108
Warts, to Extirpate..................................... 68
Water, to dry up the, in cases of gouty diseases........ 95
Water, when a person cannot hold his....................112
Weak and Dull Head......................................131
When a woman suffers from not being regular............. 86
When a person has taken a false step, how to help, etc.. 89
Windgall in horses 124
Witch, an excellent way to prove whether a person is.... 78
Witch, that no, may leave a church...................... 68
Witch, to burn a, so that she receives pock-marks....... 69
Witch, to catch a....................................... 68
Witch, to cause a, to die within one minute............. 69
Witches and Sorcery..................................... 69
Wolf's Blessing or Charm................................ 97
Womb Disease 68
Worm on the Finger...................................... 87
Worms and Colic 83, 115
Worms from the Corn, to drive...........................130
Wounds, a good ointment for.........................103, 108
Yellow Jaundice of men and women........................104

ALBERTUS MAGNUS

BEING THE APPROVED, VERIFIED, SYMPATHETIC AND NATURAL

EGYPTIAN SECRETS

OR,

WHITE AND BLACK ART FOR MAN AND BEAST

THE BOOK OF NATURE AND THE HIDDEN SECRETS
AND MYSTERIES OF LIFE UNVEILED; BEING THE

Forbidden Knowledge of Ancient Philosophers

By that celebrated Student, Philosopher, Chemist, Naturalist, Psychomist, Astrologer, Alchemist, Metallurgist, Sorcerer, Explanator of the Mysteries of Wizards and Witchcraft; together with recondite Views of numerous Arts and Sciences—Obscure, Plain, Practical, Etc., Etc.

TRANSLATED FROM THE GERMAN

CONTENTS OF VOL. III.

Recipes for Heart Blood—For Frozen Feet or Hands—When a Man or Beast Becomes Blind—An Ointment for Various Poisonous Boils and Pimples—For Arthritis of Children—How to Make a Melancholy, Dejected, Low-Spirited Man Happy Again—An Excellent Eye Water for Man and Beast—For Laboring Pains and Prolapsus—For Gun Shot Wounds, whether Caused by Iron or Lead—Wounds Made by Thorns and Briars—How to Draw Missiles from the Body Again—and many other approved recipes which have heretofore never been made public.

EGYPTIAN PUBLISHING CO.

CHICAGO.

PREFACE

The wonderful cures that have been effected by me at home and abroad, on man and beast, have caused and induced many persons to express their desire to have some of my remedies, which have proved so efficient, published. My intention, however, was not to have a great deal of my treatment of human ailments and diseases put into print, so as not subject myself to the critic and censure of the learned. For such reasons I have published in this volume but few domestic medicines for mankind, and given more space and attention to the treatment of dumb animals. For the cure of cattle, sheep, and hogs especially, though for horses, there will be found in this little book, quite a number of treatments for all sorts of diseases and injuries, whatever they may be called; also the manner of treatment of animals, when they are well, and how to prevent many injuries. All medicines mentioned herein, have been tried and proved by me, personally, during a practice of many years and have ever been found efficacious.

My heartfelt wish therefore is, that this book may prove to the reader a source of great value, and a recommendation to the author.

(Signed)

Albertus Magnus.

ALBERTUS MAGNUS
OR
EGYPTIAN SECRETS

To Quench Burning Thirst and Inward Heat.

Take a drachm of white eyestone mixed with a quart of fresh well-water and shake it until the water becomes entirely white. If it should be preferred sweet, white sugar may be added. To drink at meal times and during the day will allay the burning thirst and great heat.

For a Heated Stomach.

Take one pint of white rose vinegar, one half pound of sugar, boil these in a very clean brass pan, as long as it takes to boil a soft egg, and use it instead of salt to the meat at meal time. It is a good sauce, healthy and agreeable.

Also: Take a fresh or dried cherry into the mouth and keep the stone on the tongue, it restrains violent thirst at home and abroad. Further: The sour fibres of grape vines will also quench the thirst. Also: A piece of pectine chewed and kept during the entire day in the mouth, while traveling, is good to still the thirst.

For Feverish Thirst.

Before retiring at night, make a julep of quince roses or sorrel juice. But in lieu of these take rose sugar, and make a julep thereof, or drink milk of almonds, or eat raisins. These things will cause an easy rest and sleep, and strengthen the heart and liver. Also: The juice of currants, or a julep of strawberry juice, are excellent for quenching the thirst.

For Bronchitis.

If a person is troubled with great heat of the body, and to have bronchitis, such a person must receive attention inwardly as well as outwardly. In the first place, apply the recipe of white eyestone as given above. The mouth has to be cleaned three times per day with the domestic powder.

When bronchitis, however, has developed itself, (it may in some cases be used from the commencement of the disease,) bruise house-leak leaves, press them through a cloth, take mornings after rising, and evenings before laying down, three spoonfuls of the juice, with as much goat's milk, it will soothe the pain, and alleviate the disease.

Note.

A horse affected with this disease, feed evenings and mornings with pure oats, and give it for a drink a pail of pure water. When the horse takes its mouth out of the water, hold a clean dish under its mouth, in order to catch all the water that runs out of the mouth again, therein; this water strain through a cloth, and give to the sick two or three spoonfuls thereof, and rinse the mouth with the domestic powder. Henry de Kaltenthal has used it during war times, and became fully convinced of its curative qualities.

Another Remedy for the Bronchitis.

Take three male crabs, but no female, pound them alive in a mortar, pour three spoonfuls of white vinegar thereon, then press the juice through a cloth, and take it evenings before retiring to bed. Wet a woolen cloth therewith, rinse the mouth thoroughly with it, and gargle with such water. If it does not help at once, continue the cure for two or three days in succession.

Another Remedy for the Same Disease.

Take fresh turnips, grind them on the grater, press the juice out, and with it rinse the mouth frequently. In lieu of fresh turnips, dried ones will answer the same purpose. A handful of these boil in a quart of water, wherewith rinse and gargle the mouth and throat frequently. It does not matter if the patient should swallow some of this, it allays the heat.

Still another Remedy for the Above Disease.

Put dried quinces in fresh water, gargle the throat therewith, and let it remain awhile in the mouth. It cools and purifies well. But if such quinces can be obtained, grate them upon a grater, put them in well-water and apply as stated. The best remedy, however is the following, which may be had at all hours. Take a quart of fresh well-water, a quart of small raisins, two ounces brown rock candy, ten figs, some licorice root cut fine, and five fall roses (white are the best). Take twelve leaves of small sage, let all of these articles boil, about as long as eggs have to boil, then take it off the fire.

For the White and Bloody Dysentery.

As soon as a person notices the approach of this disease, put, wherever you have to go, two or three handfuls of salt therein, and let it stand thus over night. This do on the first day.

Also: Then take some gold filings, as much as salt is used in an egg, put into a chicken broth. It strengthens mightily. Pearls prepared for twelve hours, and as much taken thereof as salt is used to an egg, also in chicken broth, also the same quantity of corals, it strengthens and increases the appetite. Meanwhile, burn rye-bread water in the following manner:

Take rye bread, as warm as it comes from the bake-oven, break it into pieces, but do not cut it. The bread put into a distilling apparatus, and distil quickly water therefrom, the faster the better. As soon as you have gathered three spoonfuls, take it; the remainder save in a well corked phial. As soon as these breadcrumbs have been put into the flame of a coal fire, let some one else break or crumble the crusts fine, put them in a tin can, be the same large or small, just as you may desire, a smaller or larger quantity of water; then fill the pot with red wine, let it stand over night, and the next day distil water therefrom.

In case the dysentery will not cease, give of this water to an infant a few drops thereof; to a child ten years old, one spoonful, and to an adult from five to six spoonfuls per day.

When the patient becomes visibly weaker, give him daily gold, pearls and corals to take, according to directions as above. This will strengthen his heart. While the flux prevails, the strength of the patient is waning. The wine for the patient must be in accordance to his state of weakness, it must not be too much loaded with gold nor too sour or too strong.

All nourishment to be given to the patient should be of a binding nature. At the same ratio as the red flux ceases, the nourishment of a binding nature should also cease in proportion. Before a convalescent takes any food, let him first try some good old rose sugar or old quinces, and if the stomach is very sore and weak, try some old quince jelly.

If the patient feels chilly, add six spoonfuls of malvasier to this jelly. In want of this article take a good, strong, old wine. Let this boil over the fire, put it upon a piece of white leather, apply it to the navel as hot as it can be borne. Whenever the patient wishes to eat, remove the plaster, but after the meal apply it again to the stomach. This plaster is good for eight days and strengthens the stomach.

In case all the above given remedies avail nothing, or the dysentery increases rapidly, while the bread water is being prepared, take a three-finger pinch of pulvis rhei in wine or warm broth twice per day.

For Griping Pains and Straining.

Rarely ever is dysentery without griping pains or straining. In such cases the patient should have every night, before retiring to bed, a quart of warm goat's milk sweetened with sugar. The dish into which the goat's milk is to be milked, must be made warm before milking. Hence it is necessary that the goat's milk be near at hand; whenever such milk gets cold it must not be warmed. This beverage quenches the thirst, gives nourishment, heals the injured intestines, and soothes the strains. It may be drank as long as the pain lasts.

In case the griping pains do not yet cease, the patient should have three or four drops of scorpion oil rubbed over the navel. If this does not help either, then take matronis vulgaris, cut them off from the stem a span high, strip flowers and herbs from the stem, perhaps a good handful, cut them fine, add an egg thereto, also two spoonfuls of flower and three spoonfuls of vinegar, stir it well together and bake it in lard or olive oil until it resembles that of a cake. Then put it as warm as you can stand it upon the navel, and put a cloth folded four times over it. When it becomes cold warm it again in the lard or oil, as before mentioned. With God's aid this will prove beneficent.

To secure Natural Sleep and Rest.

Take oil of mace and rose salve, of one as much as of the other; mix well together; with this anoint the temples, the neck, the nostrils, the pulses on both arms, and the soles of the feet. Repeat this several days in succession before retiring to bed. It brings on the natural sleep.

How to Stop the Blood.

When a horse bleeds so hard that the blood cannot be stopped, take sour vinegar and dip the horse's nostrils therein. When a man or woman bleeds hard, let the breasts be dipped in the strong vinegar, and the blood will cease to flow.

To Stop the Blood, if the Bleeding Person is Absent.

Call the injured by his christian name, and draw a stick from a hedge above you, and the upper part below, and call again that name, then plant the hedge stick again in the ground, in the name of God the Father, the Son and Holy Ghost, Amen. Then say a Lord's Prayer, an Ave Maria and a Creed.

Another Remedy for the Same.

If a person bleeds put both his hands into cold water, if this does not help, let his hands and arms be immersed in water up to elbow and shoulder blade.

A Remedy for Nose Bleeding.

Dip a little wadding in good ink, insert it into the nose or other bleeding injuries. It will stop the blood.

For Gathered Breasts.

Take orange, nine seeds, a few drachms, and sweat, the oftener the better.

Likewise: sweet oil, aspenwood, sage, wax and ottermenig herbs and roots dried and powdered, of which a salve is to be made. Apply to a piece of leather, and lay this plaster over the milt, but should commence near the back bone and extend 'oward the stomach of the size of a hand.

Another for the Same Trouble.

Blood forget thy flow and thy go, and may the Lord forget him who utters false witness and is partial in his judgment before court, knowingly and wantonly. In the name of God the Father, the Son and the Holy Spirit. This recite three times. If it is done for a dumb animal, speak its name or put yourself close to it.

To drive away the Secundines.

Of chickwood one ounce, dissolve in warm wine is a certain and reliable remedy.

When Dropsy threatens the System.

Take three drops of amber oil in wine, and the purging will cause the dropsy to desist.

For Loose Teeth.

Take an armful of fumitory straw, wash the same clean of all impurities, bruise it in a mortar, press the juice out, put the same into a pan, boil over a slow fire and skim it well; then add as much old clarified honey thereto as there is juice in the pan, and again boil it and skim it. Draw in glass bottles. It will keep for a long time.

Of this take some to rub the gums therewith; you may also drink it; it fastens the teeth again. To add a little burnt alum would be well, in case the teeth are very loose.

A spoonful of this sap given to children having worms will drive them away.

For Gravel, Obstruction of Water in Old and Aggravated Cases. A certain Cure effected within Ten or Twelve Days.

Take herbum oviga orea, pulverize it, and give the patient every morning a tablespoonful in an egg, but let him fast after taking this for four hours, and in less than one hour the patient will urinate. If this remedy is used for ten or twelve days in succession, all gravel and stone in the kidneys will break, and pass off without pain.

How to have a nearly painless and safe Childbirth, when the natural Pains are at hand.

Take a handful of white mugwort or artemisia, a similar quantity of melissa, four ounces lavender flowers, all these herbs must be dried, four ounces galligan, four ounces cinnamon, two ounces fennel seed. All these things cut fine and pound them, afterward two pints of wine poured over it and boiled down over a quick fire; then strain through a cloth and frequently give the patient to drink. Sweeten the beverage either with honey or sugar.

N. B.—When the birth is a still-born child, add to the above drink a handful of senna and another of seventree.

An approved Remedy to carry off the Secundines.

Take salt of the size of a pea, and mace of the same quantity. These articles lay upon the right knee, and take it therefrom, with the mouth chew it and swallow it; or, it may be spit out again, then cough twice or thrice as hard as possible. If it does not pass yet, let the proceedings be repeated by placing the stuff on the left knee.

If the above remedy is not yet ample, try the following:

Take one-eighth of an ounce of amber, and one-sixteenth of an ounce of mace. These give to the patient in warm wine and a little sugar, and let them keep themselves warm.

An approved Remedy for Jaundice.

Procure from five to ten cents' worth of aniseed oil, pour from fourteen to fifteen drops in a spoonful of brandy, liquor or meat broth, and take morning before breakfast, or an equal dose before dinner, and after supper an equal quantity. When this medicine is used up the jaundice will have vanished. Probatum.

This aniseed preparation is not only an excellent remedy for jaundice, but also good for lung and other diseases, but the quantity should be increased. A man of forty-six years suffering from pulmonary disease, whom the physician had given up, considered it useless to give him any more medicine, was advised by some friend to use the aniseed cure. The patient procured forthwith two dollars' worth of aniseed at once, and within a fortnight was entirely cured, and is still alive enjoying the best of health. This oil is really a rejuvenator.

For the Jaundice.

Take a large white onion, cut the herbage therefrom, bore a hole into the bulb, put a piece of the size of a nut of teriak therein, also one ounce of powdered saffron, mix all well together and put it into the onion, and boil carefully over a fire so as not to burn it. After having boiled sufficiently long, put it in a linen cloth, press the juice well out of it. Give this to the patient mornings before breakfast to drink. It will surely cure.

To Extinguish Moles and Marks.

Take of nitre, white cream of tartar, one pinch of each, pound separately, then mix it, and after sifting put it in a deep dish until it burns up and becomes like a cake, then put it in another dish, pour water over it, stir it with the finger till it dissolves, afterward strain through a filter, pour it into a new earthen pot upon the fire, but not to boil, merely to dry and pulverize.

After this is done, take nine ounces of distilled vinegar, two ounces of brandy, put into a glass and mix the powder prepared in the above manner therewith; let it distil in the sun for three days and save it for use. In using it, wash morning and evening the moles with it, and but a few days will elapse to show the result to be a pure white skin and quite free from moles or freckles.

For Swollen Feet and Pains of the Skin.

The bark of elderberry mixed with strong salt water, should be used as a wash for sore feet and other injuries of the skin.

For Round or Maw Worms.

The juice of elderberries, mixed with honey, taken inwardly, will kill the round worms in the body, but it should be given prudently, according to the vigor and age of the respective parties.

How to Restore Nature when arrested by Cold or Ill Health.

When women are thus suffering, they should take the sap or juice of the elder bark, or, apply the bruised leaves of this shrub warm upon the body.

A Mush for the Stomach or Bellyaches of Infants.

Take one-half ounce of good rose water, the same quantity of larkspur water and curly balsam-apple, flower water, also five cents' worth of wormwood seed syrup, some five cents' worth of pulverized tragacanth. All of these ingredients must be well mixed together and sweetened with sugar, then add a little spring-water, boil it gently in a dish and let it cool off, but take care that it does not sour. Let the child eat three, but seldom as much as four. teaspoonfuls thereof.

A good Remedy for the Four Days' Fever.

Take theriak, wormwood and nutmeg, of each, one and a half drachms, and five drops of spir. vitr.

These articles carefully mixed in three spoonfuls of cardobenedict water, give two or three hours before you expect the fever to return. After taking this, drink a good gill of first class cognac brandy. Perspire after taking the dose, but be sure the patient's bowels have been opened within the last twenty-four hours.

A Splendid Eye Water.

Take white rose water, or in case that cannot be had, red rose water, and a little native camphor, five grains of white vitriol, pound into a mortar, then pour the rose water over it; shake well. Before retiring to sleep, wet a clean linen cloth in this water and rub the eyes with it. It is also good to clear the freckles of the face.

How to make a good Stomach Plaster.

Take two ounces of melted wax, in which stir a drachm of each of the following: ground cloves, nutmeg, alba cevatria and turpentine.

After straining all these articles through a cloth, add ten grains of wormwood oil, stir all well together till it becomes cold, spread it upon a piece of muslin; when cold, paint balsam of cloves over it, wherewith it may be freshened up from time to time. Apply to the stomach externally. It is a very efficacious remedy.

For Constipated Persons, how to open the Bowels within One Hours' Time.

Take a dose of salts and senna, such as apothecaries sell.

How to make a Gravel Water.

Take parsley, radishes, shave grass (horse-tail, Dutch rush), and cornelian cherries, put these together in the alembic. It is a very efficient remedy.

A good Recipe for a Person suffering from a Fall.

Give him a good draught of linseed oil to drink, also some chervil water. But in case the fall was a very violent one, give mummio and spermaceti made warm in wine vinegar. This has been used frequently with great effect.

How to distil a Water to cause a Perspiration.

Take a good handful of cardobenedict herbs, same quantity of wormwood centifolium, cut fine and put into a dish, sprinkle these well with some good old wine. Let it stand and soak for four days; then take a drachm of cinnamon, a whole lemon put into a glass, pour again good old wine over it, and let it stand again for four days, cut it into fine pieces and distil in the alembic. The result will be an excellent water for sweating the patient.

For the Cough of Infants.

Take violet roots, powdered licorice root, of each one-half of an ounce, one drachm brown bithynia root, a pinch of saffron, four ounces candy sugar (white). All these articles pound to a fine powder and mix well together. Give as much as will cover the point of a knife, whenever required.

A valuable Recipe for Pulmonary and other Consumptions, also a Drink for the Breast, a wonderful Beverage.

Speedwell (veronica), scabiosas, magwort, a handful of hyssop, sage, acremening, bethunia, blue violets, half of a handful; five ounces sweet angelica, alantis roots, licorice root, waywort, aniseed, licorice juice, rhubarb, senna, of these articles four ounces; of carraway seed and field fennel, two ounces. The dried herbs as well as the roots, must be cut fine and pounded; then pour a good quart of pure spring water over it, let it remain standing over night, then put it in a new covered pot, boil down one-half of its volume, and it will be all right and ready for use.

A good Herb Wine for a Laxative.

Take white waywort roots, three ounces of alantis roots, one and one-half drachm white nettle blossoms, one and one-half ounce benedictus roots, a stem of wormwood herbs, all together a good handful, one-half ounce of lemon peels; also of rhubarb, one-half ounce, one and one-half ounce of senna, half an ounce of prepared coriander, a few white androgenes, a little aniseed, one-half ounce violet roots, sweet angelica, one ounce of good sloe blossoms. Take for dinner and supper, in soup, a spoonful of this mixture, or take every day twice the cardobenedictus powder.

For Erysipelas.

Take of rhubarb, turbirbium and diogrite, a scruple of each. Pulverize, mix well, and take in good warm wine.

N. B.—Before taking the medicament, take the day previous a drachm of prepared cream of tartar in warm wine. Keep warm and do not go into the fresh air. Take also a warm beverage of beer or good wine with an egg beaten in, and sweetened with sugar, but eat no specified food. This will purify the blood.

Another approved Remedy for Erysipelas.

Whoever is troubled with erysipelas on the foot or any other limb, should pronounce the following, holding his face near the sores: Oh, thou all-burning and inflamed carbuncle and fiery spark, how art thou so hot, how art thou so dark, with the aid of God I seek thee, with God the Son I find thee, with God the Holy Ghost I banish thee. In the name of God the Father, God the Son, and God the Holy Spirit. While pronouncing these three holiest names, blow outwardly over the erysipelas.

A good Ointment for Serious Warts.

Make a white turnip hollow inside by taking the pit out, put fresh butter therein, also a fresh hen's egg. Let these articles be rendered by broiling inside, pour through a cloth, with a little rose water added, and boil it till it becomes the consistency of a salve. This is a very reliable ointment.

To Drive away Warts.

Speak over the warts thus: Vanish in flaming ether, salamander! Flow together, step forward, and finish thus, in the name of God the Father, God the Son and God the Holy Spirit. This must be repeated three times, and each time while pronouncing the three holiest names, blow over the warts, and in a very few weeks they will vanish, so that none will know whence they have gone to.

To Drive away the Gout and Neuralgia.

Speak thus: The bells will soon ring out and sound, the chiming out of gout and flux, that ye no longer shall my life embrace, this horrid pain is out of place, go hence, depart, be laid now in thy grave, that I no longer fear for thee may have, this grant me God the Father, God the Son and God the Holy Spirit. While pronouncing each of these holy names, make a motion with the hand over the feet, downward, and if the ailment is in both feet it must be pronounced three times over each foot. If it is a neuralgic pain, stroke with the hands outward bent over the seat of the pain.

To Extirpate Corns.

Commence by softening the corn in a foot-bath, then cut the corn as close as possible. In case of a man, wait for the funeral of a man; in case of a woman, wait for the funeral of a female; be seated in your bed-room, take off the stocking and move the index finger over the corn, and speak thus: What I touch may vanish, what I hold may depart like the dead in the tomb, in the name of God the Father, the Son and Holy Spirit. As long as the bells are tolling speak the above formula, and continue to move over the corn, and say constantly as follows: And "what I touch may vanish like the dead in the grave," three times, but always pronounce the three highest names.

For Bloodshot or Red Eyes.

Take white autumn roses, soak them three hours in aqua rosarum (rose water), then tie them over the eye, but do not expose yourself to the open air for the day.

For Marasmus for Old and Young Folks.

Take seventeen good corals, twenty-five genuine pearls, thirteen fresh arthritis grains, take the black skin from the latter, then take a stem of rosemary and the same of marjoram, a thimble full of mousear herbs, a good sized chicken stomach, all of these articles well dried and pounded fine in a mortar. Of this powder the patient may take every day three times the quantity covering the points of a table knife, in anything palatable to the sick person.

In using this powder, draw water from a brook against the stream, put therein consumption herbs and a large common field bean straw, also a handful of hazel poplar leaves and the same quantity of camomile flowers. Boil well in a new earthen pot and bathe morning and evening arms and hands therein.

An excellent Stomach Tonic.

Take of each of the following articles one-half an ounce, viz.: Orange peels, good cinnamon, mace, nutmeg, fresh violet roots, and half a drachm of white ginger, cardamon seed, white nettle blossoms, cubebs, paradies apple grains; one and a half drachms quinces, one drachm Spanish pepper and one drachm aniseed. After sweetening well with sugar, it may be taken evening and morning as a tonic for the stomach. Chicken stomachs may be added thereto as one may desire.

An Ointment for Sore Breasts.

Take a pure cold cast-lead lye three or four ounces, one point of a knife full of saffron, pure linseed oil, two or three ounces, two ounces of good vinegar, the whites of two or three eggs, these things beat together, then take rye flour, which is unbolted, stir it until it gets stiff. Take a white cloth, of the form of the breast, cut a small hole therein so that the nipple draws out, and put the salve upon a cloth and apply it to the breast till it becomes hard. When used in good season before waiting too long, it will allay the pains, but if it is neglected too long it must need suppurate, the ointment draws it open and heals it. It must not be cut or rubbed or washed.

A good Relief for a Person who met with a Fall upon the Breast.

Soon after meeting with such an accident, give the patient a good draught of linseed oil to drink, and procure from a druggist one-half an ounce of dragon's blood, take also one-half a wine glass of chervil water, one-half of the same quantity linden blossom water, mix the dragon's blood with the distilled water, warm it and let the patient drink it.

For a Youth contracting Hernia or Rupture.

Cut three bunches of hair from the crown of the head, tie it in a clean cloth, carry it noiselessly into another district (county), and bury it under a young willow tree so that it may grow together therewith. It is a sure remedy.

For a Cough.

Take violet root, pounded licorice of each one-half an ounce, brown bethynia roots, four drachms, point of a knife full of saffron, four ounces of white rock candy. All these pounded fine, and mix well together and the point of a knife full given to the patient whenever required will be beneficent.

A good Black Plaster.

Take one-half pound of olive oil, a quarter of a pound of silver litherage, a quart of good vinegar; rose vinegar would be the best for the purpose. Stir all these articles together in a pan placed upon the fire till the mass becomes black. Then pour it into pure water, and grind it upon a stone or board together. It is a good remedy for all sorts of injuries.

For Bad Hearing.

Take bell grease, such as is used in greasing the bells in belfries, and grease behind the ears therewith.

A Wash for Ladies, to obtain a fair and beautiful Physiognomy.

Take bread crumbs, put them into goat's milk whey, strain

or distil it, paint the face with it and it will become fair and beautiful.

To Facilitate Healthy Sleep.

Procure two rabbit ears, place them under the pillow of a person who cannot sleep, without his knowledge.

For Newly-Born Children.

For their first bath take one and one-half of a quart of red wine and a quart of simple peonia leaves boiled. In this fluid bathe the infants.

A good Pomatum for Sore Heads.

Take one-half of a pound of butter, such as was never watered, ginger, pepper, of each one-half an ounce, and one ounce of copper water, half an ounce of cloves, and some laurel leaves and stove soot.

All these articles pounded and mixed together, and boiled up in the butter until it is rendered completely. When it becomes cold grease the head therewith. It heals splendidly.

An Ointment for the Itch or Mange.

A glass of ordinary wine, a glass of cognac brandy, butter, hog's lard and cereat, of each one ounce, salt and pepper, bolus and a little sulphur.

For Mole and Liver Spots.

White camphor, Venetian borax, of each one ounce, bean meal, four points of a knife full, white precipitate of mercury, two ounces lemon, rose water, sugar, parsnip water, white lily water, of each one ounce, prepared saltpetre lozenges and a few grains of linseed. Distil for three days in the heat, afterward press through a cloth and put in a cool place. This will be an excellent water for liver spots. Before washing with it, add a little alum and the white of an egg, and a little of red snails, and grease therewith. It is a great medicament.

How to Beautify the Face.

In the first place take twelve or twenty-four fresh eggs, put them in a glazed pot, pour boiled vinegar over the eggs, cover this well and keep it for eighteen days in a cellar; then pour the vinegar off, soak two loaves of wheaten bread in a quart of goat's milk, then take white wort, cut fine and mix together, put all in an alembic and distil to a water.

An Ointment for the Face for Heat and Cold.

Procure one pound of bay leaves, pound them well in a mortar, boil one pound of sweet oil in a pan, afterward strain the same through a cloth, then put it again into a pan, pour seven pounds of good Spanish wine (port wine or sherry wine), one pound unwashed butter, boil all this slowly, afterward put another ounce of well pulverized incense thereto. Then take the pan from the fire, stir well together and expose it to the air in a glass vessel, so that it will thicken. Afterward the face may be anointed therewith, whenever it is required.

A Domestic Injection.

Take poplar leaves, violet stems, camomile flowers, white maple leaves, ottermenig, red oats, of each a handful; these articles boil in a pint of broth of mutton or lamb; also, one spoonful of good honey, four spoonfuls of sweet oil and the yellow of an egg.

For Straining Pains.

Take incense, mastix, viola colophony and rose water, of one as much as of the other, and let the vapors thereof go toward your person.

When a Person cannot pass Water.

Take black carraway seed, light grains of incense, of each one ounce, lay upon live coals, and inhale the fumes. It is a well confirmed remedy.

How to retain the passing Labor Pains.

According to the Pharmacopœa a tonic is made by pharmacutists called the ursuline drink. This is to be given according to direction, and all will be right.

For the After Pains.

Take linseed oil, hempseed oil, of each two ounces, and three yolks of eggs. This put into a dish and stir well together. Put on a cloth, and apply to the stomach of the patient.

For the Flooding.

Water of balm (melisses), pennyroyal water, of each one ounce, and eleven drops of carbuncle water, to drink.

For Putrid Mouths or the Scurvy.

Brunnelle water, Norway maple leaves and strawberry water. With these waters rinse the mouth clean, and with a hornscraper well scraped, roast mush meal upon a new lid, put it in rose honey and paint the mouth therewith.

A Gargle for a Putrid Mouth.

Take turnips, autumn roses, juniperberries, lancet herbs, white iron herbs, blackberry roots, of each a handful, boil in a clean pot, and with this water gargle.

How to Wean a Child without producing Pains in the Breast.

Take some hazelnut leaves, about one month old, parsley, and strew it under three different doors to the sweepings. Apply this in a new rag to the breast.

A good Powder for Marasmus of Children.

Seventeen good pearls, thirteen corals, a chicken stomach, a sprig of green rosemary, green marjoram, nine palsy grains, three sprigs of mouse-ear herbs.

A good Stomach Plaster for a Bewitched Child.

Take a little of the oil of almonds, a little deer's tallow, as much of rose vinegar and one ounce of carraway seed. All these articles pounded together, put upon a blue paper, and lay it upon the child's stomach.

But before using the plaster, the mother must, after eating supper, cut three pieces of bread thin, while sticking the knife three times through the bread, and put this knife under the child's back during the night. If the child is bewitched, the knife will be rusty all over on the next morning; then take the bread from the knife, put butter thereon, and give it to a black dog to eat, while you must put an old shirt on the child, which, after remaining for three days and three nights upon the child's person, must be taken off and interred with the above mentioned plaster. This has to be done noiselessly, before sunrise, and under an alderwood shrub.

A good Plaster for an Obscure Disease.

Assafœtida, whole saffron, a bulb of garlic, a handful of nouse leek, mixed with the white of two eggs. Put upon a cloth, and apply to the sore spot.

An Excellent Ointment for Erysipeias.

Take the flowers of St. John's herb, wool flowers, white lily leaves, red rose leaves, of each a good handful; pour one pound of sweet oil over it and distil in the sun. When preparing the ointment take two thimblefuls of oil and one of cut bees-wax and render it down in the oil, and with the ointment thus obtained grease the injury.

Another Recipe for the same Ailment.

Goat's milk, butter and saffron, rendered down and applied as a salve.

For Erysipelas.

Take eight drops of white eyestone oil (amber oil), in two ounces of elder flower water, and perspire.

A good Remedy for the Gout.

Take rendered goat's milk butter, roast cow manure therein, apply to a cloth and put upon the patient's sores.

For the Tympanitis and Dropsy.

Three ounces of aniseed, one-half an ounce of glycerine, one-half pound of raisins and one quart of old wine poured thereon. After every meal take a glassful of it.

Subcarbonate, wormwood salt, centauris salt, cardobenedictum salt, and prepared cream of tartar, of each one drachm, well mixed together. Take every morning in soup, or chicken broth, a good size knife point full thereof.

A Good Powder for the Gravel.

Crab's eyes and fir tree needles, of each one ounce, of wild briar seed, three ounces. The skin of a chicken's stomach, and prepared cream of tartar, two ounces, orange peels, four ounces, and eight ounces of brown rock candy.

Pulverize fine all these articles, and take every morning three large pinches thereof, especially when the moon is waning, and bathe often in tepid water.

An excellent Purifier for Womb Disease.

Cinnamon, cloves, mace, ginger, long black pepper, lemons, of each one drachm; sage, melisses, rue, balsam, majoram, white maple, rosemary, elder flowers, sloe blossoms, of each one handful; angelica, waywort and benedictus water, of each one ounce; wormwood, woodwort, and parsnips, of each one and one-half ounces; one lemon and one orange, with the skins, soaked in one and one-half quart of wine, and three days after this distilled in an alembic, will produce the desired extract.

To prevent that any harm may come to the Cattle.

Give them the quenching water of a blacksmith to drink.

For Loose Teeth of Cows.

Mix alum and vinegar together and rub the teeth of the cattle therewith.

When the Livers of Cows rot.

Give to the cow on St. Martin day (November 10th), a piece of quince, and during the ensuing year the liver of such a cow will not rot.

For Bewitched Cattle.

Take sabintree, pound it to powder, mix salt with it, and rub the tongue and roof of the mouth with it, and it will remain healthy.

When a Cow is plagued with Erysipelas.

Take elder blossoms and give the cow to eat and the disease will leave. Or, drive the cow upon the meadow, and pay attention where the cow treads with her right hind leg. Dig that sod out with a knife and turn it over; when it becomes yellow or withered the erysipelas will vanish.

Another Remedy for the Disease.

Take a red woolen cloth, scarlet is the best, cut it fine, and give it to the cattle to eat in bread. It helps. Also give three stems of mayflower to the cow.

Another.

Take a cup of red wine, boil a spoonful of carraway therein, and let the cattle drink it. Some hedge blossoms, of an uneven number, is also good to take—that is, three, five, seven or nine, according to the strength of the cattle.

Still another.

Take fresh fish roe, put them upon live coals, and let the cow inhale the fumes through the nose. If the cattle, in the eighth year, has many pimples and blisters on the tongue and udder, take melissa or liver herb (mandagora), heathen, wound herbs, and snake root. Put all these herbs into a pail, and pour water over them. As often as the cattle drinks thereof, fill it up again. Only every two or three days the herbs have to be renewed. Also suspend from the neck of such sick cows Easterlurlay herbs wrapped up in a cloth.

When Cattle is Plagued with too much Bile.

Take fungus of apple tree, old shoe soles, some Christian wort (such as is sold by apothecaries), and skunk cabbage, ground to powder, and at night, when the cattle receive no more food for the day, give a spoonful of this medicament.

When Cattle Swell up.

Take three roots of waywort, and let the cattle eat it.

When Cattle are Raw and Sore.

When a horse or ox is ridden raw and sore, wash the sore two or three times a day with a strong infusion of black oak bark.

How to Wean Calves.

On the third day before full moon, calves should be weaned, and you will have beautiful large cattle.

For the Worms of Cattle.

Give such an animal one teaspoonful of wormseed three times a day.

Another Remedy for the same.

Give the animal some of the green fungus, such as grows upon manure puddles.

How Madame de Vellberg had her powder prepared.

Liver herb, such as grows on oaken tree trunks, melissa, cardobenedictus powder, veronica, aspen leaves, wood herbs,

Samile's powder, snake herb, degmentes, mayflower, brown bethunias, wormwood, oak leaves, fungus of apple trees, ashes of juniper tree wood, pear tree wood ashes, walnut and grape vine ashes, ottermening, alpis roots, hoof roots, nettle seed, gunpowder, and as much salt as the above articles make altogether.

When Cattle Die suddenly.

Wash such cattle with the cooling-off water of smith shops, or such as is used by bakers before the bake oven; or arise on a Sunday morning, before sunrise, and take a sieve, reverse it, put ashes on it, and sift it over the cattle, and the lice will vanish from their skin, or take bark of a birch, and hang it around the cattle's neck.

When Cattle are Plagued by Worms in Sore Parts or Wounds.

Take hawk weed, suspend it from the sick beast's neck, and the vermin will drop from their wounds.

When Sheep Die.

Take sheep milk, mix it with water, and drench your sheep with it.

When an Animal Belches up, and the Seat of the Ailment is Unknown.

Take half an ounce of pulverized alum, mix salt with it, and give it in one dose to the cattle.

When Animals are Bilious.

Give, in good season, croton flowers to eat. It will improve them.

Another Remedy for the same Ailment.

Take three handfuls of hemp seed and the same quantity of chickweed. Give it internally, and tie linden tree peelings around their body, and the disease will stop.

When a Cow will not Purify after Calving.

Take hazelwort and herb, cut it all up together, and give it to the cow in water or wine.

Another for the same Disease.

Take one handful of wintergreen, and let the cow eat it.

Still Another.

Give the three leaves of a house-leek to the cow, and the purification will soon take place.

When Cattle cannot pass Urine.

Take a handful of parsley roots, and the herb thereof, cut fine, boil well in water or wine, and let the cattle take it.

When a Witch besets the Animals.

Take enzian, juniper berries, ashes of pear tree wood, and salt, of one as much as of the other, of aloes and almond nuts, half the quantity. Pound all pure and fine. Mix well together. After having a pail full of this powder, take a good handful of house leek, and cut it fine. Of this give to the cattle as much as may be taken between three fingers, and push it into their throats. Cut off of such cattle's tail a tuft of hair, so that it may perspire freely. This should be done during the waning of the moon, and treat the animals every morning to a fumigation with juniper berries.

Nettleseed mixed with salt is also good at all times.

For the Swellings of Beasts.

Let a man scrape from his finger nails as much as possible, and give to the cattle or horse upon bread. Probatum.

A Powder for Open and Sore Feet.

Take garden rose leaves, as well as hedge roses, either white or red, lancet shaped waywort. Make a separate powder of each, and then mix both together. Wash the injury of the cattle with it, and strew of the powder into the same. It will heal.

To cause a Cow to give plenty of Milk.

When a cow bears the first calf, give her half of an eel's tail in half a loaf of bread, or however best it may be given, and the cow will certainly give a great deal of milk.

When an Epidemic is raging among Cattle.

Take juniper berry vinegar, teriak and pulverized horse hoof roots. Of the latter article as much as the size of a walnut. Mix well in vinegar. Give the cattle this drink, and let them have neither food nor drink for three hours after taking the medicine.

EGYPTIAN SECRETS.

For the Sudden Dying of Cattle.

Faruwind roots, bruised and boiled in water, and both roots and water given to the cattle or swine, mixed with their feed. It is an excellent remedy.

For the Superabundance of Blood in Sheep or Cattle.

Take two good handfuls of red lintels (such as are used in cooking), a good handful of oaken worm meal (such as is found between the bark and the wood), a handful of pulverized bay leaves, a handful of select tormentil (the red are the best), and one-half of a salt cake. Mix all together with the sheep or cattle feed. Salt once a day, and, in aggravated cases, twice every day therewith.

For the Witches.

Take the core of a quince, and give, on St. Mary's Eve, every animal, such a core to eat.

Another for the Witches.

Give to a human being or dumb animal, on St. Martin's Eve (tenth November, c. a.), three garlic bulbs to eat.

Another Remedy for the Same Disease.

Take soot and burned bread, pulverized, and some salt. Mix together, and give to the cattle.

When Cattle have the Dysentery.

Boil a large handful of lintels, till they become very stiff, and give them to the cattle. Repeat this so long as it helps. Give also some cottage cheese.

A Powder for the Lung Rot of Cattle.

Take white wool herbs, veronica, liverwort, snakeroot, such as grows upon the trunks of oaks, cross sage, wild balsam, aspen leaves, wormwood, mengan roots, laurel leaves, juniperberries, brown bethunias, lavender (herbs as well as flowers), and ashes of grape vines and of walnut wood. All these articles pulverize. Give once a week, but in very aggravated cases, every two days, or when necessary, even twice a day; and afterward give of the following water:

A Drink.

Take lung herbs, such as grow upon oak tree trunks, wormwood, and pating herbs, of each a like quantity. Put water in a kettle or earth pot, and let these articles boil well together, and give this beverage as stated above. Such sick cattle must not drink near water where healthy animals drink.

When the Vomit rages among Cattle.

Take gunpowder, sabintree, and beech ashes, of one as much as of the other. Powder all fine. Of this give the cattle a good tablespoonful at once. This is also good for horses. When this bad disease rages, it should be given every three or four weeks once, even if the animals are well. But immediately after giving this medicine, let the animal fast for three hours.

When Cattle are Sick, and the Disease is not known.

On St. Walpurgis Day, early, before sunrise, break cowslip flowers, powder them, and let the cattle take them.

A Remedy to apply to Cows During Christmas in order to make them give plenty of milk.

Take the milk and sinew of a herring, bay leaves, saffron, and black carraway seed. Mix well together. Put it upon four pieces of bread, and give these four pieces to four different cows.

A Remedy for the Vomit.

On New Year's Day, give every animal three bay leaves, before feeding them with anything else.

What to give a Calving Cow, soon after Calving, to make her give much Milk.

As soon as she has calved, milk her. Warm two quarts of beer, but do not boil it. In this let a piece of butter or lard, twice as large as a hen's egg, be dissolved; also, a goodly portion of saffron, powdered, and one-half of a powdered quince. Let all this be drank by the cow at once, and she will give much milk.

EGYPTIAN SECRETS.

When a Cow is hard to become with Calf.

Take nine knots of an alder tree, in the spring of the year, powder them, and give to the cow upon a fresh baked piece of bread. It has been tried with success.

Remedy against all Injuries and Diseases of Horses.

Take arsenic, the size of a small pea, and oil lard, the size of a walnut. These two articles mix well together. Take a piece of leather the size of the rough or bristly part. Do not apply the plaster too thick, and let it remain upon the sore for three days and three nights. On the fourth day, take a quart of larget, and wash it out in fresh water. Take the white of one or two eggs. Mix all these things well, so that they make an ointment. Put it where the former plaster was, until the leather falls off, as it had been before. Then take the salve, with the albumen, and put a large plaster upon the other. Boil a water of heart's-ease herb and attlic, and wash it out. Then take the dry powder, and heal therewith the sore, and no rough spot will appear thereafter. Probatum! The first plaster, however, should not be left on any longer than three days and three nights, as it will eat in too deeply.

Another Remedy for Irritation and Bristles.

Take alum, copper water, snowball, verdigris, an ounce of each. Powder all these articles fine, add half a pound of lard, render it down, pour water to it, mix the above articles thereto, let them boil thoroughly, and make an ointment thereof.

Another Remedy for the same Ailment.

Pound garlic, and mix with it honey to a mush. Make a plaster of tow or oakum the size of the injured parts. Apply as hot as the horse will stand it. Let it remain for two days, then put a fresh one on again. If you notice that it heals, grease it with honey; but in case it does not heal, put more plaster on it.

Another Remedy.

Take goblins, put them into a glass vessel, and pour so much oil upon them that they will die at once. Leave it stand for fourteen days in the sun, for distillation. With this mass grease the horse's sores twice every day. They will contract holes, but that does not matter. Continue to grease, until all is healed up. But after they are healed, take erbis herbs and crab water, of each an even proportion, and wash the sores until they become dry. Take bacon, and water, and grease well.

Still another Remedy.

Procure four ounces of the herb of armatilles, powder them, and add two ounces of lime, slakened with aquafortis to a thin mush. With this ointment grease, and put the powder over the grease. Rub it well every morning with saliva. This remedy is also good for open fistula.

Another Remedy for the above Disease.

Take a potful of pigeon manure, and boil it well. Then add some vinegar. Apply as a warm poultice, mornings and evenings. After removing the poultice, put the matter again into the pot, stir it, and use as before. Such a potful of manure may be used for eight days, but after that time a fresh potful has to be procured. This is a well approved art.

When the Hoofs of Cattle fall off.

Take the leaves of cochlearia (scurvy grass), and put them into a clean earthen pot, well covered and sealed up, so that no vapors can escape. Then put it into a bake-oven, and let dry to powder. Afterward sift through a bolting cloth, until it becomes very fine. Dry the feet well with a clean dry rag, and then apply the powder. The feet must not be tied up. Repeat twice per day, as above directed.

Should the udder and teats be so sore that the skin peels off, take leaves of radishes, pound them in a mortar, press the juice through a cloth, and apply it to the udder and teat by means of a feather; but do not touch them with your bare hands.

A Grand Art to Stop the Cramp.

EDOAE † VEOAFP † BEOAEV †

This suspend to the patient till the cramp leaves.

When the Udder of a Cow is Bewitched.

Make three wreaths of corydalis, and milk through these three times toward the feet. Then give the cow these three wreaths to eat, while speaking the following words: Cow, I give thee these wreaths, thou wilt return the milk to me, in the name of God the Father, the Son, and the Holy Spirit. Amen.

When, in early spring, the cattle are driven out for the first time, push a piece of dried beef into the throat of each animal. Put a little salt on it. Such cattle will be free from erysipelas during the coming year, and also secure against the rot.

When a cow is slow to purify herself, after calving, give hazelwort, or dried leaven of the size of a hen's egg, in pure vinegar and dissolve it.

When the navel of a calf is too large, take fresh well water, put some salt into it, and wash twice a day, mornings and evenings, the navel with it. But do not rub from above or below, but only from one side to the other.

For Worms of Cattle.

Take a little earth from under the entrance to the sitting room, a little garlic and chalk, and scrape a little from a deer's antlers. Mix well together, pour a little good vinegar to it, and pour it out into the cattle. Probatum.

A Powder for the Rot of Cattle.

Procure five cents' worth of bay leaves, enzian, a little sulphur, and one cent's worth of chalk; also, ashes of pear tree wood, walnut wood, and juniper tree wood. Mix with stove soot, of one as much of the other. Let the cattle take thereof, mornings and evenings, and always, after taking the powder, let it fast for several hours.

How to Discern what ails the Cattle.

Look sharp into the animal's eyes. If the lower streak in the eye is dim and dark, the cow is dropsical. If the two middle veins are dull and dim, then it has the rot. But if the hinder-wart vein appears dim, then the animal is bilious. If they are all pure and red, then the beast is healthy and nothing ails it.

For all sorts of Palsy, be they wherever they may, for young as well as old People. An Amulet to suspend from the neck of Adults and to be laid under the Body of Infants.

Oh, palsy! oh, palsy! how painful thou art, this complaint I to our Lord must impart, and in his holy name, who suffered death on the cross innocently, N. N., palsy and gout, very death to life. Upon a green meadow he was met by St. Ann. St. Ann spake: † Palsy and gout, whither are ye going? The gout spake: We propose to enter into the body of N. N. We want to cross into his flesh and suck his blood. Then spake again the holy woman, St. Ann: † Palsy and † gout, I command ye, by the power of God, and by the great anathema, thou running palsy, thou constant gout, † thou raging gout, † thou taking gout, † thou cold gout, † thou hot gout, † thou blood gout, † thou marrow gout, † thou venomous gout, thou goutiest gout of all gouts, I hereby command and order ye, by the power of God and by the highest anathema, to return to the wild regions of mater alma, from whence ye came my limbs to lame, thence ye shall hie again, and your ransom retain, while I my usual freshness regain. † † †

Prescription for Epilepsy.

Violet water is excellent for epileptic fits, especially for children.

Water of peonies, mixed with the violet water, of each about fifty cents' worth, and taken from thirty to forty drops every morning, before breakfast, and evening, before going to bed. Give each time one ounce of it.

A good Prescription for Fractures of Men and Beasts.

Take badger lard, rabbit lard, dog's lard, comb fat, wild sow's lard, red butter, red sea oil, verdigris, wild cat lard, fox lard, snake fat, yellow salve, deer's tallow, laurel oil, sperm oil, of each five cents' worth. Mix all these articles well together, grease the fracture with it, and tie a linen over it.

An Ointment for the Fistula.

Take one pound of good bacon, one pound of saltpetre, one pound of gelder roses, and some verdigris. Pulverize all these articles fine and let the bacon melt in them. Temper all well together, and stir until it becomes cold and firm. It is approved.

For Irritable and Bristly Horses.

Take a handful of gunpowder, pound it fine, add the albumen of an egg, and unwatered butter of the size of a hen's egg. Mix well, and grease the raw parts therewith. It would be well to wash them first with a good lye.

Another Remedy for the same Disease.

One pound of good bacon, one ounce of good laurel oil, five cents' worth of hellebore, and one ounce of mercury, prepared with linseed oil. Of these articles prepare a salve, and apply to the injuries; but always wash them first right clean with a cold lye.

How to Heal Raw Flesh Spots within twenty-four hours.

In the first place, split and cut the four streaks on their feet, in the middle. Then take three ounces of powdered bay leaves, the whites of twenty eggs, two ounces of teriac, two quarts of strong wine, and boil all together to one-half of its original volume. Let the horse drink this as warm as he can bear it. Then soak a woolen blanket in cold water, cover the horse with it, and put the belly-band on, that the blanket will not fall off, and let it remain for twenty-four hours. Give it neither food nor drink during this time. After this you may ride him again, and feed carefully. This is a well approved art.

When a Horse is Sore and Oozes Blood.

Put bacon or soap into his posterior.

When a Horse Swells Up.

Take water cresses, pound it, press the juice out and mix rye flour with it to a thin mush. Apply to the swellings of the horse.

For the Swelling of a Horse's Shoulder Blade.

Take vinegar, cow's manure, salt and polermis. Make a mush of it, and paint with this twice a day.

When the Shoulder Blade is Swelled or Sprained.

Take rye bread crumbs. If this is not handy, take rye flour, soot from a bake oven, two or three spoonfuls of honey, the albumen of three eggs, two spoonfuls of polermium, and small cuttings of hemp oakum. Mix brandy and vinegar. Apply as a poultice, as warm as the horse can bear it, on a woolen cloth. Should be done soon after the swelling appears.

A Plaster for the above Swellings.

Foliage of balsam poplars, wool herbs, linseed oil, and vinumgrecum, powdered, and mixed together, and by adding goat's milk, wine and vinegar, make into an ointment. Put upon a rag, and apply warm to the horse's swellings.

When a Horse is injured by Pressure.

Take one and a half quart of good white wine, old urine, the same quantity. Boil these things together in a new earthen pot. Cover well, so that no fumes evaporate, put a handful of salt to it. Wash the injury with some fresh and pure water. Then take the boiled fluid, and sprinkle the injuries with a feather or sponge. Wash the injured part once or twice a day.

When the Shanks of a Horse are Swelled, and the Flux appears.

Take four quarts of white wine, four ounces of alum, four ounces copper water, garlic straw, herb of centifolium, rosemary sage, of all these herbs a good handful. Put into a pot, cover well so that the steam does not evaporate. Let one-third part boil down. Before applying this remedy ride the horse. But it must not be driven through water. Bathe or wash six or seven times with the above wash every other day during the summer season. Then ride it through running water stream upward for half of an hour, and fifteen days in succession, and the shanks will become right again. During the winter season, substitute firtree cones boiled in a kettle and wash for fifteen days with such water and dispense with the riding into water.

If a Horse is Injured by Pressure, Swellings or Tumors which have to be Cut.

After cutting the horse, approach to the front of the horse, tear some few hairs out under its mane, and pronounce: In the name of the Father, the Son and the Holy Spirit; then walk around the horse and take also a few hairs from under the throat and speak as before. Walk again around the horse and take some hair from the tail and pronounce the same blessing, then walk again around the horse and stand still just as you received the horse. Pray the Lord's Prayer three times, three Ave Marias and the Creed once. Now, take the hair altogether, bore a hole into a pear-tree, put the hair therein, or draw the bark, and put the hair between. Probatum!

When a Horse becomes Scabby.

Take agrimonium and flee herbs and lard, of one as much as of the other. Put all these things into a new pot and cover well, so that no fumes evaporate. Expose to a strong flame and burn it to powder. Put of native alum and sulphur, an even quantity, pulverize and mix these altogether. Whenever you wish to use this, take for one horse a handful of the alum and sulphur powder, and an equal part of the powder made of the burned herbs, also white rosin, three cents, pound of butter or lard, one pound of bacon. Put all these articles into a pan, melt together as long as is necessary to cook a mush. Apply this as warm to the horse as your hand will bear it, rub it well into the skin. But before applying stir all thoroughly, otherwise the best will remain upon the bottom. Keep the horse dry, but do not cover it. Continue this until the horse is healed. The herbs should be gathered on the thirtieth day of the month.

When a Horse's Urinary Organs are Obstructed.

Tie parsley roots under its snout, or put some olive oil in a spoon or into the hand, and pour into the sick animal's ear.

A Plaster that will cause Suppuration and which Heals.

Take rye bread, and three or four times the quantity of salt to it. These two articles put into a pea soup which is not larded. Make a thick mush of it and apply to the injuries.

When a Horse has the Itch or an Old Sore.

Put valerian and toothwort into a pot of water. Give this to the horse to drink until the sores heal. Then take cabbage leaves and fernwort, cut and mix together, and mix a spoonful with the fodder whenever you feed the horse.

When a Horse cannot pass the Urine.

Take good wine and a goodly portion of beef's suet, warm these, wash the organs of the horse therewith as warm as your hand can bear it.

To purify the Urine.

Take attic boiled in water, and give it to the horse to drink. Then take aspen leaves, grind it to powder, and then mix with the feed of the animal.

For the Jaundice of Horses.

On the night of St. Martin's Day, and on the morning of the same day, give to the horse early red barley to eat, and during the same year the horse will not suffer from yellow jaundice.

For the Colic.

The disease is discovered thus: When a horse becomes sick and drops the head and often rises by starts, or when it prior to the days of labor pains draws the hips in, or lays down its head, etc., then these are signs of colic. Take teriac, saffron and good wine, mix well and let the horse drink it warm. Then ride it gently around and cover it well.

For Erysipelas, etc., of Man and Beast.

Wild fire, wild brand, flux and pains, coagulated blood and gangrene, I embrace thee, the Lord our God embrace thee, he is the sublimest being, who alone is able to drive away wild fire, wild brand, flux and pain, coagulated pain and gangrene as well as all other injuries. † † †

For the Gripes and Colic of Horses and Cattle.

Gripes and colic I bless ye to-day, on this sacred day, that ye from horse or cattle pass away. † † † Then take a handful of chimney soot, one handful of ashes of juniper-tree wood and a pint of good old wine. Warm it, and pour out for the animals to drink.

For Yellow Knots.

Take fodder, liver of sulphur and wormwood, of one as much as of the other, and let the horse take it in a drink, every time three points of a table knife.

When a Horse is Restive.

Take wood, such as has been struck by a thunderbolt, make a whip of it, and scourge and flog the horse therewith, and the ailment will vanish.

When one of the Eyes of a Horse threatens to get Blind.

Take wagon grease of a wheel that has been run, grease the eye-skin of the horse with it. It helps, and will contribute greatly to the healthiness of the eyes.

For the Colic of Human Beings.

Take of rosemary, marjoram, bolay, nugwort, melisses, of each three sprigs, all with the blossoms steeped in good old brandy. Take one, two or even three spoonfuls thereof. If it will not cease, take from the upper hole of a bake-oven three knife points full of soot, rub gently to fine powder, and take in a spoonful of brandy.

For the Cataract in Horses' Eyes.

Take one ounce of goose grease, one ounce of virgin honey, then strain it, half drachm saffron, half an ounce pounded orange peels, one drachm of pulverized ginger. All this mix well together, and once every day put a little into the horse's eyes.

How to discover the Disease of a Horse.

Take one ounce of venitian, teriac, boar's root, angelica and orange peels of each two ounces; pulverize all these articles fine. Give it in a pint of wine to the horse. The horse should also be bled under the tongue and ridden.

An excellent Eye Water for Man and Beast.

Fennel water, eye-bright herb water, water of sulphate of zinc, water of linden blossoms, coxspun, of each one ounce. Well mixed and shaken, and the eye washed therewith.

When a Horse is Restive.

Give it valerian roots to eat.

When a Horse is Constipated.

Draw a feather through honey, and rub the hinder part of the horse with it. The horse will be well forthwith.

When a Person is wounded by Gun-Shot, whether by Iron or Lead, or if a Thorn or Splinter is sticking in the Flesh, how to Remove it.

Roots of pimpernella, wash and roast in St. Mary's butter, pour warm on a cloth, moistened with fresh water and you will obtain an ointment, which apply to a linen cloth and place upon the injured spot, and the missile will ooze out. Leaves of balm or mother herb may also be mixed with this salve.

For Labor Pains or Falling of the Womb.

Cut a rabbit's liver into small pieces, roast them well upon a turn spit, then powder it in a mortar, mix one ounce of white sugar, one ounce of ginger, one ounce of cloves, all of which must be pulverized. Give the patient one-half an ounce, and no more, upon bread to eat, or give it in a drink. This has often been tried with great satisfaction.

When a Horse is Charmed or Bewitched.

This will be discerned when the animal constantly sweats, retains the food or hay a long time in the mouth; for this take: Fern leaves, Roman camomile, dill, of each one ounce, ground to powder, and without any danger burn and pulverize one ounce of fish bones, one ounce of wood, such as floats upon running water, and must be obtained before sunrise. All these articles well mixed and in three different motions poured out into one quart of wine vinegar, no matter at what hour or time. Whenever the horse is to take this drink, take a bone of a dog, and hang it under the right side of the horse's mane. By this usage the charm will cease and eventually subside.

When a Cow is Constipated.

Take some bees'-wax, melt it and pour it into one pint of warm milk, stir it well, then beat four eggs, yolks and whites together, and give to the cow all at once.

For the Spleen or Milt Disease.

Boil the following articles well together: one egg, one pint of wine, a little juniper salt, angelica, a little pepper, saffron, a little of the powder of alcion herbs, from one to three pinches of rasped hartshorn, and given to the cattle as warm as possible. Under the throat will appear a swelling, which must be greased with good brandy and saffron, and a ring must be made around the swelling, of saffron and brandy. Also open the swelling and wash it out with brandy and saffron.

A sure Remedy for Bristly Horses.

Take five cents' worth of each, of copper water and blue prepared vitriol, and half of this quantity of alentis. Put all of this in two quarts of fresh water and wash the horse's injuries morning and evenings with this. After this take some alum, and burn it upon an old spoon, also burn some grape vines to ashes, and an old shoe likewise. Sift it through a fine sieve. Afterward take the alant and the latter two articles, and the horse is washed with the above water, strew some of the powder upon the injured parts. If this is done in the morning the horse must rest afterward for one hour before using it for work. In the evening do as well as it will suit the case.

For the Lung Rot of Cattle.

Take of alantis wort, five cents; verdigris, five cents; saltpetre, five cents; cream of tartar very little, red bolus, sternutative powder, blue vitriol, white vitriol, dragon's blood, grey sulphur, bay leaves, Spanish pepper. All these ingredients well mixed together in wine vinegar and poured into the nostrils. For a large animal use a large tablespoonful each time. For a calf, half that quantity.

For Decayed Lungs of Cattle.

Of cognac brandy and sweet oil, one glassful, saffron, four knife points full, teriak, four knife points full, white chalk gunpowder, the same quantity. When the ailment is not very severe, give it in two different doses, but in an aggravated case, in three doses. Put it into the nostrils. It is a most excellent remedy for the disease.

For Biliousness.

Before feeding the cattle in the morning, give them a handful of oats, and nothing more for one hour. This will take the bile off. Fumigate morning and evening as follows: Woodworm, rue, assafœdita, juniper berries, juniper wood, garlic, black tobacco, put all these articles into an old earthen pot, under which coals are burning, and let the fumes go directly under the nostrils of the cattle and fumigate over belly and back. Probatum.

Another Remedy for too much Gall.

In the year 1203 the bilious fever raged in a certain place, when it happened that a man traveling with a jug of brandy, entered a stable and poured some brandy into a glass, and spoke thus: Good morning, ye brethren, your health, ye brothers, and drank the brandy all up, and gave to every animal of this brandy till the jug was emptied. His cattle was thus saved, while all the other stock in town died. Probatum.

For the Thrush of Cattle.

Rub the thrush of the animal with a slice of bread on which a little salt is sprinkled. Afterward it must be well rubbed with vinegar, salt and garlic, a little pepper may also be added. Should a hole be eaten in, put blue vitriol (copperas) into it and grease then with honey.

For the St. Anthony's Fire.

Flush I seek thee with God the Father, flush I seek thee with God the Son, flush I seek thee with God the Holy Spirit. I drive thee away in the name of the Holy Spirit. † † † Three times recited.

When Cattle have Thrush in their Mouth.

Take black rock oil, turpentine, sperm oil, of each a like quantity. Grease from two to three times per day.

An Ointment for various kinds of Pimples and Boils, also for Small-Pox, etc.

Take some unwatered butter, raw bees'-wax, pitch, saffron, for five cents, some sulphur; the sulphur must be melted in a pan, afterward add the wax, pitch, saffron, and last the butter, let it boil well together, as long as a soft egg, or till it foams over. Put it upon a rag and tie as warm as it can be borne upon the pimples and kept tight by means of another band. This is an excellent thing for poisonous eruptions of all kinds. Probatum.

For the Fits of Children.

Take five cents' worth of marine glue, of which a lozenge is to be made, and between eleven and twelve o'clock is to be laid into a child's cap. On the third day thereafter at the same hour it is to be taken away, then powdered, and give to the child every day thereof some little into the child's food, and the disease vanishes. Probatum.

For the Bad Hearing of Horses.

Take horseradish and salt, pound it well in a mortar, and the sap pressed out, and a few drops poured into the ear of the horse. It is also good for man.

To make a sad person mirthful, when the Ailment is caused by the blood.

Storkbill herbs, bolus and rue, of one as much as of the other, and make into a powder. Of this give the patient a spoonful every day. It strengthens him, and he will be happy again.

For Frozen Hands or Feet.

When feet are frozen, or a person has other frozen limbs, let them mix turpentine with salt till it becomes a salve. This apply twice a day regular for several days in succession to the frozen parts. It is an efficacious remedy.

When Cattle has a Felon on its Foot.

Burn copperas upon a brickstone and apply to the sores. It will heal fast.

For a Heavy Cough, originating from the Kidneys.

Take bacon and garlic, let these render down together, apply to the back near where the kidneys are situated, three or four times while being near the stove.

When an Animal treads into a Nail.

Take antimony and butter, mix it together, and grease the wound with it, and in forty-eight hours it will be better.

For the Womb Disease or Colic, when the Patient is not Present, and the Name of the same is only known.

A deer's antlers and a slice of rye bread, also a glass of red wine shall for N. N.'s colic and womb be very fine. Womb and blood, womb remain good, or thou wilt bring flesh and blood to the grave. In the name of God the Father, the Son and the Holy Spirit. Recite three times. Probatum.

For the Heart Blood.

Three lillies are growing upon thy heart, the first is named God the Father, the other God the Son, the third. God's will I command the heart blood stand still. In the name of God the Father, God the Son and God the Holy Spirit. This and the name of the patient repeat three times, and lay the hands with the thumbs cross-wise over each other.

For the Swelling up of Cattle.

Put the right arm across the cattle, the left one under it where you stand, and speak: What I with my right arm surround, may it not break and bound; in the name of God the Father, God the Son, and God the Holy Spirit. Three times repeat.

Blood Stopping.

For an injury either caused by stabbing or cutting, an approved stopping of the blood is, to let thirty or forty drops of oil of turpentine trickle into the injury.

For the Cataract in the Eyes of a Horse.

Take green spiderwort, give it to the horse with its food for a period of fourteen days and it will cease.

For Cancer.

Mix ottermening and goat's gall together, and grease the impurity with it. If it is the worm, boil walnut leaves in vinegar and use as a wash.

For Obstruction of the Urine.

Take iron herb water, five cents; wild cherry, five cents; dragon's blood and selterswater; mix all and give the patient to drink.

How to make Wild Game and other Animals Stand.

Upon our Lord's heart, three roses stand, the first called kindness in every land, the other called blossom, the third called deer (or whatever animal it may be, call its name), stand still. No more than our Saviour from the cross ran away, no more shalt thou from the place leave to-day, till I myself bid thee thither to leap, by the four elements of heaven I order thee to stand, forbid thee to stand, forbid thee to jump, leap or crawl over the sand; tragta, gramontetta, angtela. † † †

When a Man or an Animal is in Danger of getting Blind.

Speak thus: There sat three poor blind persons upon the street of God, then speak our beloved Lord Jesus Christ: Ye poor blind folks, why sit ye here? We sit here, because we cannot see the Almighty and may not know him. Then spake again our beloved Lord Jesus Christ with his mouth and breath: I will bless you all for your fiery brand, and bless you for weapon and arms, for white and for yellow, for fall and cut and for nails, that he may depart, like Judas left the garden, and that man left who did the rope wind, wherewith the wicked our Saviour did bind when he was bound upon the cross. I know not what has befallen thee that be thy ransom for the sake of Christ. Blow three † † † into the eyes, in the name of God the Father, the Son and the Holy Spirit.

For a Fractured Leg of a Horse, when the Injury is of a recent Occurrence.

Take new fresh water, one pound of rosin, wallwort and toothwort, all pounded and well mixed, and then wax and rosin stirred in until it becomes an ointment. Of this put upon a linen cloth and tie while warm over the horse. After this proceed to shingle the fracture. Let the plaster remain for three days, and then renew the painting of the leg.

When a Horse Falls upon or wrenches his Backbone.

Hie thee to a graveyard and procure a skull, put it into fresh water in a wooden vessel, and let the horse drink three weeks therefrom, and it will become well again. Then take the head of the dead again to its place from whence you took it.

To Heal Proud Flesh.

Take the sap of nettles, grease the injury therewith, also dry nettles to powder. It is an approved remedy, dries and heals also neuralgic pains.

How to Prevent a Horse from Contracting the Glanders, a Well-Approved Piece of Art.

To accomplish this take the following articles: Iron herbs, green juniperberries, wall rue, of each two handfuls, bacon, turnips, lung-wort, bay leaves, speedwell (veronica), of each of these three handfuls, coriander fifteen ounces, enzian sixteen ounces. All these articles must be well pulverized, and every third day in the morning give to the horse a small handful of it with its feed, which must be moistened with the following water: Gipsy wound herbs, swallow roots, the large specie of fern roots, catnip, mugwort, verbena, enzian, of each three handfuls. Put all these herbs in a cloth, and then into a tub of running water; with it moisten the food and let the horse drink of it every day. These herbs should be often renewed.

For all Sorts of Injury of Horses under the Saddle.

Waywort roots should be tied over the injury when suppuration oozes out. Let him eat the roots, and you may use the horse for riding without trouble.

An Ointment for the Eyes of Horses.

Take three ounces of leaf lard, one spoonful of honey; in case the eye is inflamed and looks reddish, take as much as the point of a knife of ginger; in case the eye is not red, take half of that quantity of pepper, and grease the eyes with ointment. But if no inflammation is noticeable, take only the lard and honey to anoint.

When a Horse Leans its Head to One Side, it is an Indication of the Worm in the Ear.

Take fresh bacon, add wine and vinegar, let this boil well, and put it into the horse's ear lukewarm.

For Bony Excrescences of Horses.

Make a dough of fine wheat flour, put this as a poultice upon the horse's leg for a period of three days. If the spavin is still open on the fourth day, open the bandage, and apply hog manure, wheat flour with saliva upon the injury and let this remain three or four days, and the spavin will be released from the true bone.

To Prevent a Traveler from Ill Befalling Him.

If it is a rider on horseback, say: Rider of good cheer; if a foot traveler, say: Hero, cheerful be and good, we have partaken of Christ's own blood. God in heaven is my shield, the earth is my shoe, greet thee God my man, if thou art stronger than God, come on and attack me, thou art not able to fetter me, not able to stab me, thou canst not hit me, because God the Lord does prevent, who to me his aid has lent. God the Son is with thee, God the Holy Spirit of the union three, stands between us very close and hard, that in peace and happiness we may part. † † † This must be recited three times in succession, and no one will harm the traveler.

When the Cow Loses her Milk, how to Cause its Return.

Of such a cow obtain a pot full of milk, pour such in three different times into a running water stream upward in the three highest names. It must be used three times—morning, evening, and again morning.

A Good Way to Stop the Constipation of Cattle.

Take three handfuls of peas, let them be well cooked, so that the shell falls off, then take some olive oil, some butter, two ounces of good soap, one spoonful of beef marrow; let all these boil well together, pour a pot full of milk to it, and give it to the cattle as warm as it can bear it.

A Good Salve for the Eyes.

Take vitriol of the size of a pea and dissolve in soft water in a phial. Apply morning and evening to the eye.

When a Horse does not Eat.

Rub its teeth well with pepper and garlic, and it will soon eat again with great appetite. It is a good remedy.

Remedy against the Biting of Rabid Dogs.

The St. Petersburgh Miscellaneous Essays for the Science of Pathology, volume of 1511, relates the following: Morachetti, operator in a hospital in Moscow, who, while sojourning in the province of Ukrain, was requested one day to render medical aid to fifteen persons, all of whom had been bitten by a mad dog. While he was preparing for the necessary arrangements, there appeared a committee composed of several old persons, who came to beseech the doctor to permit a certain peasant to attend to the unfortunate patients, since this peasant had obtained a great celebrity for many years, by his successful healing of hydrophobia.

The prayer having been granted, the peasant gave to fourteen of the sick a strong decoction of sumit and fl. genista luteæ tinctoriæ, (one and one-half of a pound daily), and examined them twice daily, under their tongues, where, as this farmer said, little knots would form containing the poisonous matter. As soon as these knots in reality appeared (of which Dr. Marochetti convinced himself satisfactorily), they were opened and cauterized with a red hot needle, whereupon the patient had to gargle his throat with the decoction of the geniate. The result of this was, that the fourteen, (of which only two, which had been bitten last, did not show these knots), were discharged after six weeks' cure in an entirely healthy condition.

A little girl, however, the fifteenth of the bitten party, who had been treated in the usual way, was attacked on the seventh day by hydrophobia, and died eight hours after its appearance. Those who had been thoroughly cured, Dr. Marochetti saw three years afterward and all of the fourteeen were hale and hearty.

Five years after this occurrence, Dr. Marochetti had occasion to verify this important discovery in Podolia. He was entrusted with the treatment of twenty-six persons who had been bitten by a rabid dog. The sick were composed of nine men, eleven women and six children. A decoction of genista was forthwith prepared and the attentive examination of the tongues resulted as follows: Five men, all the women and three children showed the mentioned little knots, those who had been severely wounded, already on the third day, the others on the fifth, seventh and ninth day respectively. One patient, a woman, who had received but a slight bite on the leg, showed only on the twenty-first day, the appearance of the knots. Even those seven on whose tongues these knots never appeared continued to drink the decoction for six weeks and all of them were cured. These knots must, however, be opened within twenty-four hours of their appearance, or the poison may return to the other parts of the body, and the patient would thus be helplessly lost.

An Art, how to Quench Fire without Water.

Inscribe the following letters upon every side of a plate, and throw it into the fire. It will go out of itself.

```
S A T O R
A R E P O
T E N E T
O P E R A
R O T A S
```

A Preventive, which must be carried upon the Body, for the Arts and Wiles of Gypsies.

Just the same as the prophet Jonah, the prototype of Christ had been provided for during three days and three nights in a body of the whale, so may the Almighty God protect me against all danger with his fatherly kindness. J. J. J.

How to fix a Thief so that he must stand still. This grace should be pronounced on a Thursday in the morning before sunrise, under the canopy of Heaven.

Ye thieves, I hereby conjure ye, that ye may be obedient, the same as Christ was obedient to his Heavenly Father till he was put upon the cross; and ye shall stand still for me and not depart from under my eyes; in the name of the Trinity, I order ye by the power of God and the incarnation of Jesus Christ not to go from hence, † † † like Christ the Lord stood on the shores of Jordan, when St. John baptized him. Thus I conjure thee, horse and rider, that ye will stand for me and not leave from under my eyes, like Christ our Lord was steadfast, when fastened on the cross, and redeemed the patriarchs and all mankind from the powers of hell. Ye thieves, I bind ye, like Christ the Lord bound hell, thus are ye fettered, ye thieves. † † † with those works ye were bound and fixed, I again release you all.

An Extraordinary quick Banishment.

Thou rider and footman ye come from thence, under your hat you are sprinkled with the blood of Christ, and by his holy five wounds your rifle, gun and pistol be bound. Sword, dagger and knife are banished and bound, in the name of God the Father, the Son and the Holy Spirit. This must be spoken three times.

Dissolved again.

Rider and footman, when I conjured ye at this time, depart from hence in the name of Christ, by God's own word, and Christ our Lord depart in peace for ever henceforth.

How to cause a Thief to return Stolen Goods.

Proceed early in the morning, before sunrise, to a pear tree, and take three nails from a bier, or nails of a hoof which have never been used, and hold up the nails toward the rising of the sun, and speak as follows:

O, thief! I fasten thee with this first nail! I fasten it into thy brow and skull, that what thou hast stolen thou must return to the place from which it was taken. Thou shalt feel so sick and so sad, at that place where thou hast committed the theft, like the disciple Judas felt when he betrayed Jesus. The other nail, which I into thy lung and liver will fasten, that thou to return the plunder will hasten, thou shalt feel so sick and feel so woe, that it will attract thee to that place to go, just like Pilate does feel the pangs of hell. The third nail thief, which into thy foot I hammer and burn, that the stolen things thou at once wilt return to the very place from whence thou hast stolen them. O, thief! I bind thee and compel thee, by these three nails, which had been thrust through Christ's holy feet and hands, to return all thou hast taken. † † † The nails must be greased with lard of penitent sinners.

To be given to Cattle against Witchcraft and Diabolical Mischief.

```
S A T O R
A R E P O
T E N E T
O P E R A
R O T A S
```

To prevent a Wound from Hurting.

Speak thus: The wounds I bind in three names, that thou will retain, flame, water, marasmus, and swelling, in the name of the Holy Trinity. This must be recited three times. Then move with a thread three times around the wound, put it into the right corner toward the sun, and speak: I there put thee, that thou wilt attract gouty water, dropsy, and suppuration, and all what may be injurious to the wound. † † † Amen. Recite the Lord's Prayer, and trust in God.

How to stay the Pains of a Fresh Wound.

Our beloved Lord Jesus Christ had many boils and wounds, but never had them bound. They do not become sore, they fester not, neither do they suppurate. Jonas was blind, when I, the heavenly child, said unto him: As true as the holy five wounds were inflicted, and did not curdle nor fester. From them I take water and blood, that is for all hurts and injuries good. Holy is the man who can heal all wounds and all injuries. † † † Amen.

An Art, how to Stop the Blood, which is good at all times.

As soon as you have cut or hurt yourself, speak: O, blissful wounds! O, blissful hour, blessed is the day when Christ was born, in the name of † † † Amen.

An Amulet to carry on your Person.

Carry these words with you, and no one will be able to assail you: Agania, Azaria, and Misael, praise ye the Lord, for He has redeemed us from hell and rescued us from death, and preserved us in the fire. Therefore may the Lord prevent the fire against us.

I.
N. I. R
I.

A Preventive from all Harm from Weapons.

Jesus, God and man may protect me. N. N., against all arms and weapons, short or long of range; for all metal and material retain thy fire, like Mary kept their purity, before as well as after. Christ bind up all guns, like Jesus bound up humanity in meekness. Jesus exhort all arms and weapons, like Mary, the mother of God, was secured against sin. Thus may the three drops of blood which Christ perspired on Mount Olivet. Jesus Christ protect me against manslaughter and burning fire. Jesus, let me not die, and, much less, not be confounded and damned, without partaking of the holy sacrament. So help me God the Father, Son and Holy Spirit, Amen.

Security from Firearms and Animals.

Jesus traveled through the Red Sea, and beheld the land; hence must break all fetters and band. Break and become useless all guns, rifles, cannons and pistols. All false witnesses become silent. The blessing God hath given, while creating the first of mankind, may come over me for all times. The blessing given to Joseph in his dream, that Mary, with Jesus, should flee into Egypt, may this blessing cover me forever. Holy and lovely be the † in my right hand, thus I journey over the entire land, where no one will be robbed, killed, and betrayed, and no one will ever be waylaid. That no one will harm me, and no one can charm me, no dog to bite, no wild beast to fight me, from all this protect my flesh and my blood, though especially for sins and false witnesses and slanderers' tongues, which reach from earth toward the very gates of heaven. By the power of the four Evangelists, in the name of God the Father, God the Son and the Holy Spirit. Amen.

A perfect Security against Shot.

The peace of our Lord Jesus Christ be with me, N. N. Oh! shot stand still, in the name of the mighty prophets Agtion and Elias, and kill me not, Oh! shot, stay, stand still! I conjure thee, by heaven and earth, and by the will of the judgment day, that thou wilt not insult me, I being a child of God. † † † Amen.

Rejecting Ball and Bullet.

The heavenly and holy trumpets, they blow away all bullets, missiles and misfortunes from me. I fly under the tree of life, which beareth twelve different kinds of fruit. I stand behind the holy altar of the Christian church. I commend myself to the Holy Trinity, which concealed N. N. behind the Corpus Christi. I commend myself to Christ's holy wounds, that no man's hands may capture me in bonds; that I may not be hit, nor shot, nor stabbed, nor thrown; neither assailed or injured, or wounded by any one; that help me, N. N., who this little book carries on his person, who is secure from all his foes, be they visible or invisible. He, too, who carries this book ever with him, cannot die without the corpse of Christ, nor can such person drown in any water, nor burn in any fire, and no unjust verdict will ever be rendered against him. To this end, help me † † †

How to Heal the Broken Legs of Sheep or other Animals.

Fractured leg, I bless thee this very day, as now the dear Lord, the Father, as now the dear Lord the Son, as now the dear Lord the Holy Spirit will order it. Wholesome be this hour, when our beloved Lord Jesus Christ was born. Now I take this hour, and over this wound I cover, that this broken leg may not swell nor fester till the mother of God, shall have another son. † † †

For such a broken leg, the following plaster must be used: Some good gunpowder, made fine, leaven, half the size of an egg, and the whites of two eggs. Stir and beat together, and apply over the wound. It is approved.

For the Cough.

Take juniperberries, sugar bread and wormwood. Cook together, and apply warm over the stomach.

How to Free Yourself of all Ropes and Fetters.

Just as the Son was obedient to the Father unto his death on the cross, thus protect me, the eternal God to-day, by his rose-colored blood, through his holy five wounds, which he received upon the cross, just so I must be loosened and blessed, as the cup and the very heavenly bread which Jesus offered unto his twelve disciples on Holy Thursday. Jesus crossed the Red Sea, and saw the land, hence shall break all fetters and bands. Broken be all arms, weapons, and missiles become dull and useless.

The blessing which God bestowed when he created man may come over me, N. N., at all times. The blessing God rendered unto Joseph when he fled with Mary and Jesus into Egypt, be it with me forevermore, that I may be worthy and good. The cross is my right hand, wherewith I travel the open land, that I may not be waylaid and robbed, nor whipped, injured, or hurt in any way. Thus protect me, God, all my flesh and blood, from evil hours and from false tongues no less such as reach from earth to heaven, through the power of holy Evangelist St. John, in the name of † † †

When a Person goes out to Battle, and speaks the following, he will be Secure against Swords and other Weapons which may be Drawn against him.

God greet ye, brothers of good cheer. Ye have drank of Christ's blood. This I have drank for your own good. God the Father is with me. God the Son, he is with ye. God the Holy Spirit be between us two and be with us all that no one be able to draw the sword from the hilt. Lord Jesus I am thine. I lean myself upon the help of God the Father. † † † I commend myself to the sweet name of Jesus Christ who is above me.

As true as the Lord liveth and soars above, so true will his holy angels protect me with his love and protect my going in and coming out, hither and thither. God the Father be my power. God the Son be my strength. God's holy angels defy and chase all my foes and all bands of thieves, and protect me against all ills and grievances. As sun and moon stood still at Joshua's command, when he fought the Philistine's on Jordan's strand. Three roses stand upon the dear Lord's brow, the first is kind, the second is meek, the third is his divine will, whoever is under it must stand fixed and still. † † †

A Protection for all who carry this Blessing with them. They will possess a Grand Secret which no other being will understand.

Christ, in the midst of peace, went with his disciples abroad. St. Matthew, St. Mark, St. Luke, St. John. The Four Evangelists protect me, N. N., by the everpraised majesty and unity of God. J. J. J. Amen. I. C. V. J. I. R. 3, 121, be with me at all distances. † † † Amen.

How to Shoot Securely.

Take the heart of a bat, and the liver at that, and mix it with the lead when thou doth bullets cast, and thou will shoot all things dead. Take a skull, and place the die under it, pour the lead through the eye-holes into the mould, and with such bullets and balls shoot. Probatum!

To Prevent Mice from doing any Injury in Barns, Bins and Stables.

Mark well, when you harvest the corn, or whatever it is, and when you bring the first load home, and while putting the first sheaves into the barn, take the same into your right hand and speak: Here I place for man his bread, but mice and vermin be it death. In the name of God the Father, and the Son and the Holy Spirit.

A good Way to Fix Thieves.

Three lilies stand upon our Lord's holy grave. The first is God's courage, the other God's blood, the third God's will.

Thief, stand still. No more as Jesus Christ descended from the †, shall thou from this spot depart. That I command in the name of the four Evangelists and the four elements of heaven, whether in water or by shot, before court or face to face, that thou remainest affixed. Stand still, scapegrace. Stand still, till all the stars of heaven I behold, and the sun darts its rays, whether warm or cold. Thus I forbid thy leaping and running. This I order thee, thief stop thy ways so cunning, in the name † † † Amen. This must be spoken three times.

When the Urine of a Person is Mixed with Blood.

Take three spoonfuls of sweet oil, boil it in a little earthen pot filled with wine. Drink it for three days, it will surely help. Or, boil juniperberries in water, give it to the patient for several days morning and evening. It is a sure cure.

How to remove Neuralgia in Arm or Foot by a Vapor Bath.

Take juniper tree sprouts, wild lettuce, oak tree sprouts, speedwell, alant roots, onions and camomiles. Boil these articles in water, and apply repeatedly as a poultice over arm or foot, and they will remove neuralgia from the limbs.

To secure Children against Jaundice, Rheumatism and Epilepsy during their entire Lifetime.

Powder the part known as the core in the centre of a leg of young lamb or mutton, and mix an equal quantity (by weight) of hipscratch to it, and let it be taken in milk or in mush, and the young ones will be ever free of the ailment.

To Stop Sanguinous Discharges.

Take hartshorn, scrape it, and burn it to powder, mix dried fennel seed also powdered. Give the powder to drink in rain-water, and the result will be achieved.

N. B. Do not take too much hartshorn, so that it does not stop too quickly.

To Prevent Children having Measles from becoming Blind.

As soon as the children get sick from measles, hang on their necks the roots of purnellac, and your sorrows may cease. Probatum.

How to Draw out a Thorn or Splinter.

Take carrots bruised with honey and make a powder thereof. Put over the injury, it will draw the substance out and soothe the pains.

For Aches in Back and Loins.

Take the roots of wool herbs, pound it to powder, put the same into wine, and let it stand for twenty-four hours. After this, boil the wine and drink half of an ounce of it each time. The backache as well as the pains of loins will never trouble you again.

For Cramp in the Stomach.

Take a handful of hipptree seed pods, boil them soft in a pint of water, and drink this tea, or cook them with dried prunes, and eat them repeatedly.

When a Person has the Gravel.

Take the seed of wild rose apples, acorns, and red hazelnut blossoms, grind them to powder and drink this mixed with wine.

That no Wolf or Dog may Bite or Bark at You.

Speak the following: Thus did it happen, on a Friday it was, when our Lord God rode over a field of grass, he carried neither money nor purse with him; for he owned naught but his five holy wounds. May God protect us against wolves, dogs and hounds, he gave to St. Peter the keys for the locks, wherewith to close the jaws of wolves and of dogs. In the name of † † †

MISCELLANEOUS PARCHMENTS, CONSISTING OF RARE, OLD MANUSCRIPTS FOUND AMONGST THE EFFECTS OF ALBERTUS MAGNUS, AND SUPPOSED TO HAVE BEEN WRITTEN BY HIM.

Of Magical Suspensions and Alligations; showing how, and by what power they receive Virtue, and are efficacious in Natural Magic.

When the soul of the world, by its virtue, does make all things (that are generated, or artificially made) fruitful, by sealing and impressing on them Celestial Virtues for the work of some wonderful effect, then things themselves not only applied by collyry, or suffume, or ointment, of any other such like away; but when they are conveniently bound to, or wrapped up, or suspended about the neck, or any other way applied, although by ever so easy a contract, they do impress their virtue upon us: by the alligations, etc., therefore, the affinities of the body and mind are changed into sickness or health, valor, fear, sadness or joy, and the like; they render those that carry them, gracious, terrible, acceptable, rejected, honored, beloved, or hateful and abominable.

Now these kinds of passions are conceived to be infused no otherwise than is manifest in the grafting of trees, where the vital life and virtue is communicated from the trunk to the twig engrafted in it, by way of contact and alligation; so in the female palm tree, when she comes near to the male, which the gardener seeing, he binds them together by ropes across, but soon becomes straight, as if by the continuation of the rope she had received a propagating virtue from the male. And it is said, if a woman takes a needle, and bewray it with dung, and put it up in earth in which a carcass has been buried, and carry it about her in a piece of cloth used at a funeral, no man can defy her as long as she carries it.

Now, by these examples, we see how, by certain alligations of certain things, also suspensions, or by the most simple contact of continuation of any thread, we may be able to receive some virtues thereby; but it is necessary to know the certain rule of magical alligation and suspension; and the manner that the art requires in this, viz.: that they must be done under a certain and suitable constellation; and they must be done with wire, or silken threads, or sinews of certain animals; and those things that are to be wrapped up, are to be done in the leaves of herbs, or skins of animals, or membraneous parchments, etc. For, if you would procure the SOLARY virtue of anything, this is to be wrapped up in bay leaves, or the skin of a lion, hung round the neck with gold, silk, or purple or yellow thread; while the sun reigns in the heavens, so shalt thou be endured with the virtue of that thing. So if a saturine quality or thing be desired, thou shalt in like manner take that thing, while Saturn reigns, and wrap it up in the skin of an ass, or in a cloth used at a funeral, especially if melancholy or sadness is to be induced, and with a sad, or ash, or leaden, or black silk of thread, hang it about thy neck; and so in the same manner we must proceed with the rest distinctly and progressively.

Of Antipathies; of Actives and Passives; of Stones, Fishes. Rivers, etc., of the Wonderful Celestial and Terrestrial Influences, Etc.

It is necessary, in this place, to speak of the antipathies of natural things, seeing it is requisite, as we go on, to have a thorough knowledge of that obstinate contrariety of Nature, when anything shuns its contrary, and drives it, as it were, out of its presence.

Such antipathy as this has the root rhubarb against choler; molasses against poison; the sapphire stone against hot biles, feverish heats, and diseases of the eyes; the amethyst against drunkenness; the jasper against the bloody-flux and offensive imaginations; the emerald, and *agnus caftus* against lust; achates, or agates, against poison; poiny against the falling sickness; coral against the ebullition of black choler, and pains of the stomach; the topaz against spiritual heats, such as are covetousness, lust, and all manner of love excesses.

The same antipathy is there, also, against the dandelion against the herb organ, and the wing of a bat, and the heart of a lap-wing, from the presence of which they fly. Also the organ is contrary to a certain poisonous fly which cannot resist the sun, and resists salamanders, and loathes cabbage with such a deadly hatred that they cannot endure each other. So they say cucumbers hate oil. And the gall of a crow makes even men fearful, and drives them from it with horror.

A diamond disagrees with a loadstone; that being present, it suffers no iron to be drawn to it. Sheep avoid frog-parsley as a deadly thing; and what is more wonderful. Nature has depicted the sign of this antipathy upon the livers of sheep, in which the very figure of frog-parsley does naturally appear. Again, goats hate garden basil, as if there was nothing more pernicious.

And, amongst animals, mice and weasels disagree; so a lizard is of a contrary nature to a scorpion, and induces great terror to the scorpion with its very sight, and they are therefore killed with oil; which oil will likewise cure the wounds made by scorpions. There is a great enmity between scorpions and mice; therefore, if a mouse be applied to the bite of a scorpion, he cures it. Nothing is so much an enemy to snakes as crabs; and if swine be hurt by them, they are cured by crabs: the sun also, being in Cancer, serpents are tormented. Also, the scorpion and crocodile kill one another; and if the bird Ibis does but touch a crocodile with one of his feathers, he makes him immovable. The bird called a bustard flies away at the sight of a horse; and a hart will bound forward at its greatest speed at the sight of a ram, or a viper.

An elephant trembles at the hearing of the grunting of a hog; so does a lion at the crowing of a cock; and a panther will not touch them that are anointed with the fat of a hen, especially if garlic had been put into it. There is also an enmity between foxes and swans; bulls and jackdaws. And some birds are at a perpetual variance, as daws and owls; kites and crows, turtle and ring-tail; egepis and eagles; also, harts and dragons. Amongst water animals, there is a great antipathy between dolphins and whirlpools; the mullet and pike; lamprey and conger; pourcontrel and lobster, which latter, but seeing the former, is nearly struck dead with fear; but the lobster tears the conger. The civet-cat cannot resist the panther; and if the skins of both be hung up against each other, the skin or hairs of the panther will fall off.

Apollo says, in his hieroglyphics, if any one be girt about with the skin of a civet-cat, he may pass safe through his enemies. The lamb flies from the wolf; and if the tail, skin, or head of lupus be hung up in the sheep's cot, they cannot eat their meat for very fear. And Pliny mentions the bird called the marlin, that breaks the eggs of the crow, whose young are annoyed by the fox; that she also will pinch the whelps of the fox, and the fox likewise, which, when the crow sees, they help the fox against her as against a common enemy. The linnet lives in, and eats thistles; yet she hates the ass, because he eats the thistles and flowers of them. There is so great an enmity between the little bird called esalon and the ass, that their blood will not mix; and that, at the simple braying of an ass, both the esalon's eggs and young perish together.

There is, also, a total antipathy of the olive-tree to the harlot; that, if she plant it, it will neither thrive nor prosper, but wither. A lion fears lighted torches, and is tamed by nothing sooner. The wolf fears not sword or spear, but a stone; by the throwing of which a wound being made, worms breed in the wolf. A horse fears a camel so much that he cannot endure a picture of that beast. An elephant, when he rages, is quieted by seeing a cock. A snake is afraid of a naked man, but pursues one clothed. A mad bull is tamed by being tied fast to a fig-tree. Amber attracts all things to it but a garden-basil, and things smeared with oil, between which there is a natural antipathy.

Of the Occult Virtues of Things which are Inherent in them only in their Lifetime, and such as Remain in them even after Death.

It is expedient for us to know that there are some things which retain virtue only while they are living, others even after death. So in the colic, if a live duck be applied to the belly, it takes away the pain, and the duck dies. If you take the heart out of any animal, and, while it is warm, bind it to one that has a quartan fever, it drives it away. So if any one shall swallow the heart of a lapwing, swallow, weasel, or a mole, while it is yet living and warm with natural heat, it improves his intellect, and helps him to remember, understand, and foretell things to come.

Hence, this general rule: That whatever things are taken for magical uses from animals, whether they are stones, members, hair, excrements, nails, or anything else, they must be taken from those animals while they are yet alive, and, if it is possible, that they may live afterward. If you take the tongue of a frog, you put the frog into water again; and Democritus writes, that if any one shall take out the tongue of a water-frog, no other part of the animal sticking to it, and lay it upon the place where the heart beats of a woman, she is compelled against her will, to answer whatsoever you shall ask of her. Also, take the eyes of a frog, which must be extracted before sunrise, and bound to the sick party, and the frog to be let go again blind into the water, the party shall be cured of ague; also, the same will, being bound with the flesh of a nightingale in the skin of a hart, keep a person always wakeful.

Also, the roe of the fork fish being bound to the navel, is said to cure bowel pains, if it be taken from it alive, and the fish put into the sea again. So the right eye of a serpent being applied to the soreness of eyes, cures the same; if the serpent be let go alive, and afterward let go, cures the toothache; and dogs will never bark at those who have the tail of a weasel that has escaped. Democritus says: that if the tongue of the chameleon be taken alive, it conduces to good success in trials, and likewise in love affairs.

There are many properties that remain after death; and these are things in which the idea of the matter is less swallowed up, according to Plato, in them even after death, that which is immortal in them will work some wonderful things— as in the skins we have mentioned of several wild beasts, which will corrode and eat one another after death; also, a drum made of the rocket-fish, drives all creeping things at what distance soever the sound of it is heard.

Of Sorceries—Their Wonderful and Truthful Power—Of Witchcraft, Etc.

The force of Sorceries are, no doubt, very powerful; indeed they are able to confound, subvert, consume, and change all inferior things; likewise there are sorceries by which we can suspend the faculties of men and beasts. Now, as we have promised, we will show what some of these kinds of sorceries are, that, by the example of these, there may be a way opened for the whole subject of them. Of these, the first is a certain kind of blood, which, how much power it has in sorcery, we will now consider:

First, if it comes over new wine, it will turn it sour; and if it does but touch a vine, it will spoil it forever; and, by its very touch, it renders all plants and trees barren, and those newly set, die; it burns up all the herbs in the garden, and makes fruit fall from trees; it makes dim the beauty of polished ivory, and makes it rusty; it likewise makes brass rusty, and to smell very strong; by the taste, it makes dogs run mad, and, being thus mad, if they once bite any one, that wound is incurable; it destroys whole hives of bees, and drives them away, if it does but touch them; it makes linen black that is boiled with it; it makes mares cast, by touching them with it; it makes asses barren, if they eat of the corn touched by it. The ashes of clothes when cast upon purple garments, that are to be washed, change their original color, and likewise take away the color and fragrance of flowers.

It also drives away tertian and quartan agues, if it be put into the wool of a black ram, and tied up in a silver bracelet; as also if the soles of the patient's feet be anointed therewith, and especially if it be done by the person (him or herself), the patient not knowing what she uses. It likewise cures the falling sickness; but most especially it cures them that are afraid of water or drink after they are bitten by a mad dog, if only such a cloth be put under the cup. Likewise, if a person shall walk with it in their hand, before sunrise, in a field of standing corn, all hurtful things perish; but if after sunrise, the corn withers; also, they are able to expel hail, rain, thunder and lightning; more of which Pliny mentions. Know this, that if they happen at the decrease of the moon, they are a much greater poison than in the increase, and yet much greater if they happen between the decrease and change; but if they happen in the eclipse of the sun or moon, they are a most incurable and violent poison. But they are of the greatest force when they happen in the first years, for then if they but touch the door-posts of a house, no mischief can take effect in it. And some say that the threads of any garment touched therewith is hard to burn, and if they are cast into a fire, it will spread no farther. Also it is noted, that the root of piony being given with castor, and smeared over with such a cloth, it cureth the falling sickness.

Again, let the stomach of a hart be roasted, and to it be put a perfume made with a cloth of this kind; it will make cross-bows unless for the killing of any game. The hairs of a camel, put under dung, breeds serpents; and if they are burnt, will drive away serpents with the fume. So great and powerful a poison is in them, that they are a poison to poisonous creatures.

We next come to speak of hippomanes, which, amongst sorceries, are not accounted the least; and this is a little venomous piece of flesh, the size of a fig, and black, which is in the forehead of a colt newly foaled, which unless the mare herself does presently eat, she will hardly ever love her foals, or let them suck; and this is said to be a most powerful philter to cause love, if it be powdered, and drunk in a cup with the blood of him that is in love; such a potion, it is supposed, was given by Medea to Jason.

The civet-cat, also, abounds with sorceries; for the posts of a door being touched with her blood, the arts of jugglers and sorcerers are so invalid, that evil spirits can by no means be called up, or be compelled to talk with them—this is Pliny's report. Also, those that are anointed with the oil of her feet being boiled with the ashes of the ankle bone of the same and the blood of a weasel, shall become odious to all. The same, also, is to be done with the eye being decocted. If any one has a little of the strait-gut of this animal about him, and

It is bound to the left arm, it is said to be a charm for all true love affairs, and to withstand witchcraft.

We next come to speak of the blood of a baslisk, which magicians call the blood of Saturn. This procures (by its virtues) for him that carries it about him, good success of petitions from great men; likewise makes him amazingly successful in the cure of diseases, and the grant of many privileges. They say, also, that a TICK, if it be taken out of the left ear of a dog, and be altogether black, if the sick person shall answer him that brought it in, and who, standing at his feet, shall ask him concerning his disease, there is certain hope of life; and that he shall die if he makes him no answer. They say, also, that a stone bitten by a mad dog causes discord, if it be put into drinks; and if any one shall put the tongue of a dog, dried, into his shoe, or some of the powder, no dog is able to bark at him who has it; and more powerful this, if the herb hound's tongue be put with it. And likewise, dogs will not bark at him who has the heart of a dog in his pocket.

The red toad (Pliny says), living in briers and brambles, is full of sorceries, and is capable of wonderful things; there is a little bone in his left side, which being cast into cold water, makes it presently hot; but which, also, the rage of dogs are restrained, and lovers' quarrels disposed of, if it be put in their drink, and makes servants faithful and serviceable.

On the contrary, the bone which is on the right side makes hot water cold, and it binds so that no heat can make it hot while it there remains. It is a certain cure for ague if it be bound to the sick, in a snake's skin; and likewise cures all fevers, the St. Anthony's Fire, and restrains unholy desires. And the spleen and heart are effectual antidotes against the poisons of the said toad. Thus much has Pliny written.

Also, it is said, that the sword with which a man has been slain possesses wonderful power; for if the snaffle of a bridle, or bit, or spurs be made of it, with these a horse ever so wild is tamed, and made gentle and obedient. They say, if we dip a sword with which any one was beheaded, in wine, that it cures the chills and fevers, the sick being given to drink of it. There is a liquor made, by which men are made as raging and furious as a bear, imagining themselves in every respect to be changed into one; and this is done by dissolving or boiling the brains and heart of that animal in new wine, and giving any one to drink out of a skull, and while the force of the draught operates, he will fancy every living creature to be a bear like to himself; neither can anything divert or cure him till the fumes and virtue of the liquor are entirely expended, no other distemper being perceivable in him.

The most certain cure of a violent headache, is to take any herb growing upon the top of the head of an image, the same being bound, or hung about one with a red thread, it will soon allay the violent pain thereof.

To Cause several kinds of Dreams.

Now we will endeavor to show how to cause pleasant, sad, or true dreams. But that we may more certainly effect it, it will be good first to know the causes. The meat in concoction must be corrupted (this must be taken for granted) and turned into vapors; which, being hot and light, will naturally ascend, and creep through the veins into the brain; which being always cold, condenses them into moisture, as we see clouds generated in the outer world; for by an inward reciprocation, they fall down upon the heart, the principal seat of the senses. In the meanwhile, the head grows full and heavy, and is overwhelmed in a deep sleep. Whence it comes to pass, that the species descending, meet and mix with other vapors, which make them appear preposterous and monstrous; especially, in the quiet of the night. But in the morning, when the excrementious and soul blood is separated from the pure and good, and become cool and allayed; then pure and unmixed, and pleasant visions also appear. Wherefore, I thought it not irrational, when a man is overwhelmed with drink, that vapors should arise participating, as well of the nature of what he has drank or eat, as of the humors which abound in his body, that in sleep he should rejoice or be much troubled; that fires and darkness, hail and putrefactions, should proceed from cholera, melancholy, cold and putrid humors. So to dream of killing any one, or being besmeared with blood, shows an abundance of blood; and Hippocrates and Galen say, We may judge a man to be of a sanguine complexion by it.

Hence, those who eat windy meats, by reason thereof, have rough and monstrous dreams; meats of thin and small vapors exhilarate the mind with pleasant phantoms. So also the outward application of simples, does infect the species while they are going to the heart. For the arteries of the body, says Galen, while they are dilated, do attract into themselves anything that is next them. It will much help too, to anoint the liver; for the blood passes upward out of the stomach by evaporation, and runneth to the liver; from the liver to the heart. Thus the circulating vapors are infected, and represent species of the same color. That we may not please the sleepers only, but also the waking, behold.

A Way to Cause Merry and Funny Dreams.

When you go to bed, eat balm, and you cannot desire more pleasant sights than will appear to you—fields, gardens, trees, flowers, meadows, and all the ground of a pleasant green, and covered with shady bowers; wheresoever you cast your eyes, the whole world will appear pleasant and green. Bugloss will do the same, and bows of poplar; so also oil of poplar. But

To Make Dark and Troublesome Dreams,

we eat beans; and therefore they are abhorred by the Pythagoreans, because they cause such dreams. Phaseoli, or French beans, cause the same; lentiles, onions, garlic, leeks, weebine, dorcynium Picnocomum, new red wine; these infuse dreams, wherein the phantoms are broken, crooked, angry, troubled; the person dreaming will seem to be carried in the air, and to see the rivers and sea under him; he shall dream of misfortunes, falling, death, cruel tempests, showers of rain, and cloudy days; the sun darkened, and the Heavens frowning, and nothing but fearful apparitions. So by anointing the aforesaid places with soot, or any dusty matter, and oil (which I add only to make the other enter the easier into the parts), fires, lightnings, flashings, and all things will appear in utter darkness. These are sufficient.

To Soften the Teeth, and to make them Sound and White.

Macerate the leaves of mastick, rosemary, sage, and bramble, in Port wine; then distil it with a gentle fire through a retort; take a mouthful of this, and stir about, till it turns to spittle; it fastens the teeth, makes them white, and restores the gums. The root of pellitory bruised, and put into the teeth, takes away the pain; so does the root of henbane.

Of the Wonders of Natural Magic—Sympathetic and Occult.

Some of the wonders of Magic we mean to display. But here we hasten to investigate by what means, instruments, and effects, we must apply ACTIVES to PASSIVES, to the producing of rare and uncommon effects. Therefore, to begin with things more simple: If any one shall, with an entire new knife, cut asunder a lemon, using words expressive of hatred, contumely or dislike, against any individual, the absent party, though at an unlimited distance, feels a certain inexpressible and cutting anguish of the heart, together with a cold chilliness and failure throughout the body;—likewise of living animals, if a live pigeon be cut through the heart, it causes the heart of the party intended, to become affected with a sudden failure;—likewise fear is induced by suspending the magical image of a man by a single thread; also death and destruction by means similar to these; and all these from a fatal and Magical Sympathy.

Likewise the virtues of simple animals, of which we shall speak. The application of hare's fat pulls out a thorn;—likewise any one may cure the toothache with the stone that is in the head of the toad. Also, if any one shall catch a living frog before sunrise, and he or she spits in the mouth of the frog, will be cured of an asthmatic consumption—likewise the right or left eye of same animal helps blindness; and the fat of a viper cures a bite of the same. Black hellebore easeth the headache, being applied to the head, or the powder snuffed up the nose in a moderate quantity. Coral is a well-known preservative against witchcraft and poisons, which, if worn around children's necks, enable them to combat many diseases. Paracelsus and Helmont both agree that the toad has a natural aversion to man, and his idea of hatred he carries in his head and eyes, and throughout his whole body; that the toad may be prepared for a sympathetic remedy, disorders, such as the Chills, Epileptic Fits, etc., and that our terror and natural hatred be more strongly imprinted in the toad, we must hang him in a chimney by the legs, and set under him a dish of yellow wax, to receive whatever may come down, or fall from his mouth; let him hang in this position, in our sight, for three or four days, at least till he is dead; not omitting to be present in sight of the animal, so that his terror and hatred of us may increase even to death.

A Good Plaster for Swelled Fingers.

Bacon rue, curly leaved sage, of each a little, and a squill or sea onion cut fine and mixed, and used as a poultice.

When a Horse is Stubborn while being Shod.

Speak into his ear: Casper raise thee † Melschior bind † and Balthasar entangle thee † † †

When a Cow will not be cleansed after Calving.

On Easter Evening when bells are ringing, tear grass up by the roots, and pick it up, and give such grass to the cow to eat, and it will be all right again.

How to Raise a Cow Calf and not a Bull Calf.

Take some of the cow's blood while she calves, and put it under an apple tree; the cow will bear a cow-calf the next time.

When Cattle are Dying of Knavish Tricks.

Take hazelnut roots, boil them in water, and pour into the throat of such cattle.

When during a Wet Season, Cows Eat Moist Grass and become Rotten and Threaten to Die.

Put a little ashes of juniper-tree wood into vinegar and give it to the cattle, it will lessen the gall, prevents the rot, and keeps them alive.

How to Discover whether Cattle are Troubled with Witches.

In such a case the hair bristles up against the head, and they sweat much by night or toward morning.

Against Milk Thieves.

Take hazel poplar and lay them under the doors and gates through which the cattle goes in and out, and no one will steal milk away from you.

Another Preventive for Same.

Give to a cow, while she calves, oak leaves mixed with her food and drink, and during that year no one will steal milk from your cows.

INDEX TO VOL. III.

After pains, for the..156
An Amulet to carry on your Person.......................186
Arts and Wiles of Gypsies, a preventive against.........183
Bad Hearing, for...154
Back and Loin, for aches in...............................191
Backbone, when a Horse falls upon or wrenches his......180
Back Plaster, a good......................................154
Ball and Bullet, rejecting................................187
Banishment, extraordinary quick...........................184
Beasts, for swelling of...................................162
Bilious, when Animals are.................................161
Biting of Rabid Dogs......................................182
Blind, to prevent Children having Measles, from becoming.191
Blind, when a Man or Animal is in danger of getting......179
Blood, how to stop the.........................145, 178
Blood, when the urine of a person is mixed with.........190
Bony excrescence of Horses................................181
Breast, a good Relief for a Person who met with a Fall
    upon the 154
Breasts, a remedy for gathered............................145
Bristly Horses, remedy for................................175
Broken Legs of Sheep, etc., how to heal...................187
Bronchitis 141, 142
Burning Thirst and Inward Heat, to quench.................141
Cancer 178
Calf, when a Cow is hard to become with...................165
Calves, how to wean.......................................160
Cataract in Horses' Eyes, for.............................173
Cattle are dying of knavish tricks, when..................185
Cattle are plagued with too much Bile, when...............160
Cattle are plagued by Worms in sore parts, when..........161
Cattle are Sick, and the Disease is not Known, when......164
Cattle are troubled with Witches, how to discover whether.162
Cattle cannot pass urine, when............................167
Cattle Dying suddenly 161, 163
Cattle, how to discern what ails the......................167
Cattle, swelling up of...............................160, 178
Cattle, to prevent any harm coming to the.................159
Cattle, when an Epidemic is raging among..................162
Charmed or Bewitched, when a Horse is.....................174
Childbirth, nearly painless 147
Children, for newly-born 155
Colic 172

Constipation of Cattle 181
Constipated Persons 150
Constipated, a Horse 174
Consumption, Receipt for 150
Corns, to extirpate 152
Cough, for a 154, 177, 188
Cough for Infants, for the............................150
Cows, for Loose Teeth of..............................159
Cow Calf, and not a Bull Calf, how to raise...........203
Cows eat Moist Grass, and become Rotten, when.........203
Cows to give plenty of Milk, a Remedy to apply to.....164
Cow will not be Cleansed after Calving, when a........161
Cramp, a good art to stop the.........................166
Die, when Sheep 161
Diseases of Horses, Remedy against all................165
Drink, a 164
Disease of a Horse, how to discover...................173
Dysentery 143, 163
Dropsy threatens, when 146
Eat, when a Horse does not............................182
Epilepsy, Prescription for 168
Erysipelas 151, 158, 159
Eye of a Horse, to get Blind..........................173
Eye, Salve for 182
Eyes, bloodshot 153
Eyes of Horses, Ointment for the..............178, 180
Eye Water 149, 173
Face, an Ointment for.................................156
Face, to beautify the 155
Fall, one who suffers from............................150
Feverish Thirst 141
Firearms and Animals, Security from...................186
Fire without Water, how to quench.....................183
Fistula 168
Fits of Children 177
Frozen Hands or Feet..................................177
Fractures of Men and Beasts...........................168
Fresh Wounds 185
Flooding 157
Four Days' Fever 149
Gall, a Remedy for too much...........................176
Glanders, to Prevent a Horse from contracting the.....180
Gout and Neuralgia 152
Gravel, Powder for the........................158, 181
Gravel and Obstruction of Urine, certain cure for.....146
Gravel Water 150
Griping Pains, etc 144
Gun-shot, when a Person is wounded by a...............174

INDEX TO VOLUME III.

Heart Blood 178
Heated Stomach, for a 141
Hernia or Rupture 154
Herb Wine for a Laxative, a good 151
Hoofs of Cattle fall off, when 166
Horse is Stubborn while being Shod, when a 203
Ill Befalling Him, to prevent a Traveler from 181
Injection 156
Injury of Horse under the Saddle, for the 180
Irritation and Bristles, a Remedy for 165, 166
Itch or Mange, an Ointment for the 155
Jaundice, an approved Remedy for 147, 148
Jaundice, how to secure Children against 190
Labor Pains, how to retain the passing 156, 174
Liver of Cows Rot, when the 159
Lung Rot of Cattle, a Powder for the 163, 175
Madame de Vellberg's Powder 160
Marasmus for Old and Young Folks 153, 157
Maw or Round Worms, for 148
Mice from doing Injury in Barns, etc., how to prevent 189
Milk Thieves 204
Milk, to cause a Cow to give plenty of 162
Milk, when a Cow loses her, how to cause its return 181
Mirthful, to make a Sad Person 177
Miscellaneous Parchments 192
Moles and Marks, to extinguish 148
Nail, when an Animal treads on a 178
Nature, when arrested by Cold, etc. 148
Neuralgia in Arm or Foot, how to Remove 190
Nose Bleeding, a Remedy for 145
Obscure Disease 158
Pains, for Straining 156
Palsy, for every description of 168
Perspiration, to distil Rain-water to cause 150
Pomatum for Sore Heads, a good 155
Pimples and Boils, an Ointment for various kinds of 176
Pressure, when a Horse is injured by 170, 171
Protection for All who Carry it 189
Proud Flesh, to heal 180
Putrid Mouths or the Scurvy, for 157
Raw and Sore, when Animals are 160
Raw Flesh, how to heal 169
Restive, when a Horse is 173, 174
Ropes and Fetters, how to free yourself from 188
Rot of Cattle, a Powder for the 167
Sanguinous Discharges, how to stop 190
Scabby, when a Horse becomes 171
Secundines, to drive away 146, 147

INDEX TO VOLUME III.

Shoot securely, how to.................................189
Shot, a perfect security against......................187
Sheep or Cattle, superabundance of Blood in.........163
Sleep and Rest, to secure natural....................145
St. Anthony's Fire 176
Sore and Oozing Blood of Horses and Cattle...........169
Sore Breasts, an Ointment for........................153
Spleen or Milt Disease 175
Stolen Goods, how to cause a Thief to return.........184
Stomach, for Cramp in the, etc.......................149
Stomach Plaster Tonic, how to make a.........149, 153
Suppuration, a plaster that will cause..............171
Swells up, when a Horse..............................169
Swollen Feet and Pains of the Skin..................148
Swords and other Weapons, how to secure a person
    against 188
Teeth, for loose 146
Thief, that he must stand still, to fix a.......183, 189
Thorn or Splinter, how to draw out a................191
Thrush of Cattle 176
Tympanitis and Dropsy, for the.......................124
Udder of a Cow is Bewitched, when the...............167
Urinary Organs are obstructed, when a Horse's.......171
Urine to purify 190
Urine, when a person cannot pass the................179
Vomit among Cattle 164
Warts, to drive away.................................151
Wash for Ladies to obtain fair and beautiful complexions..154
Wean a Child without Pains in the Breast, how to....157
Weapons, a Preventive from all Harms of.............186
Wild Game and other Animals stand, how to make.....179
Witch besets the Animals, when a....................162
Witchcraft and Diabolical Mischief, against.........185
Wolf or Dog may bark or bite at you, that no........191
Womb Disease, an excellent purifier of.........159, 178
Worm in the Ear 181
Worms of Cattle, for............................160, 167
Wound from burning, to prevent a....................185
Yellow Knots 173